Complete Book of
Curtains, Drapes & Blinds

First published in the United Kingdom in 2009 by
Collins & Brown
10 Southcombe Street
London
W14 0RA

An imprint of Anova Books Company Ltd

ISBN 978-1-84340-505-4

A CIP catalogue for this book is available from the
British Library.

10 9 8 7 6 5 4 3 2 1

Reproduction by Mission Productions, Hong Kong
Printed and bound by Craft Print International Ltd,
Singapore

Keep updated. Email sales@anovabooks.com
for FREE email alerts on forthcoming titles.

This book can be ordered direct from the publisher.
Contact the marketing department, but try your
bookshop first.

www.anovabooks.com

Complete Book of Curtains, Drapes & Blinds

Design ideas for every type of window treatment

COLLINS & BROWN

Contents

How to use this book...

This is a bumper book of ideas for window coverings. I know for sure that it will solve all your window problems and maybe a few others along the way! If you know my Sketchbooks – and most decorators have at least one of them in their library – then you will know that my books are just filled with ideas for window coverings. These are always in the form of black line sketches – this way you can see the design clearly – and there are very few words. My books are not really for reading, they are there to lead you through the complicated business of selecting the right curtain or blind for a particular style of window.

The problem these days is that there is so much to choose from. Never have there been so many poles and finials on the market, never have the fabrics been so colourful and the prints so inspiring, the textures so touchable. It must seem daunting to be faced with so many choices when all you want is a simple pair of curtains – and this is where my book comes in. Everything that you need to know about selecting the best fabric, the correct pole and the right style for almost any window type is clearly shown in these pages. If you want to see what the design will look like in your colour scheme, then colour it yourself just like a painting book.

Chapter One is all about getting started. Here you will find information on making an initial plan of action, creating the perfect colour scheme and choosing the right general style of curtain or blind for many different window situations. This section also has information about the different types of fabric that will be suitable for window coverings, and suggests how each could best be used.

Chapter Two covers all the essential information that will help you make your initial choices. In this chapter you will find everything you need to know about the different curtain systems currently on the market. It also looks at some of the finial designs available for curtain poles, and the basic variations for curtain and valance headings, and for pelmets.

In Chapter 3 we are looking at those little finishing touches that will make your curtains extra special – trimmings, ropes, tassels, tie-backs and hold-backs. Most of the basic types are illustrated here, although each will come in an endless selection of colourways and with some minor variations. At the end of this chapter you will find a selection of full curtain illustrations, which will give you some great ideas as to how the trimmings and other finishing touches can be used to make your curtains unique.

In the next chapter we move on to headings. The heading you use will set the style of your curtain, so it is vital that you spend some time here to choose exactly the right design for your room. All the different heading types are featured actually on a curtain, valance or pelmet, with the correct curtain system in place, so you can really get an idea of the full effect you might be able to achieve.

Chapter 5 covers a range of curtain designs. Here we look at both traditional and modern styles, using swags and tails, how to treat bay windows, Italian stringing, dress curtains, and some options for voiles. The captions highlight the main elements that are creating the look, so you will find it easy to understand how to get the same kind of effect yourself.

Of course some windows are just not suitable for curtains, so in Chapter 6 we look at some other options for window treatments. In this chapter you will find information and illustrations covering panels, café curtains, portières, difficult windows and other window dressing ideas.

If you are more interested in blinds, go to Chapter 7. Again there are clear illustrations of all the basic blind types: Roman; Austrian; Linen fold; Cascade; Oriental; and London. In addition, this chapter also covers lambrequins and shutters, including wooden Venetian blinds and blinds for Velux® windows.

In the bedroom the curtains are often coordinated with the bed, so in Chapter 8 you will find some design ideas for many different bed styles, as well as a host of options for children's rooms.

Choosing exactly the right accessories can make all the difference to an interior design scheme. In Chapter 9 we look at some of the main accessories you could use, such as table covers, screens, cushions, throws, rugs and even flowers.

Finally, in Chapter 10, you will find the basic skills and techniques needed to create most of the curtains and blinds shown in this book. There are entire books on curtain and blind making so this skills section cannot be completely comprehensive, but it will certainly allow you to make most of the designs yourself.

When you have chosen a couple of designs you think might work in your room, try colouring them up in the colours of the fabrics you will be using to see the full effect. You don't have to be an artist to do this, so don't be afraid! You can also try mixing and matching elements – although with the choice available in these pages I would be surprised if there wasn't something exactly right...

Getting Started

Design plan…

Whether you are an interior designer or a homeowner, the best advice anyone can give you before you tackle a new design project is: take your time; make a list of the basic essentials. Ask yourself a few questions… Do you have a clean slate or must you work around furniture that you already have, even if you don't really like it? Is your choice of fabric dependent on the colour of your carpets? Do you have enough money to do the job properly, or will you have to make compromises? This may lead to some hard decisions, but it is essential to consider all these things at the start – if you begin without a plan you can go around in circles and that will work out expensive in the long run.

First, decide what sort of feel you want to achieve in the room – spacious and minimal with a loft feel, perhaps, or country cosy with a homemade look. Then look at what you are working with and how you could achieve the feel you want. For instance, perhaps the room is north-facing with cold light, or the ceilings are tall so it seems unfriendly. You can change the feel in the north-facing room by choosing a warm-toned fabric, perhaps with a texture, and emphasize those tall ceilings by selecting a fabric in a cool colour, such as aqua or lime green, to give a feeling of airiness and space.

The first consideration in any interior design scheme is generally the flooring. If you need to keep the existing flooring find a spare piece if possible, so you can include it in your colour board. If you can start from scratch, have plain wood floors or a neutral carpet and cover with simple rugs, which can easily be changed when you want a different look. Rugs these days are wonderful and not that expensive.

The next priority is your furniture and how it will fit in with your new design. Sometimes existing furniture doesn't work with a different colour scheme and it can be costly to buy new. There are ways to minimize the effect of existing items of course – you could use throws to cover them up, or have them reupholstered. However, sometimes a clean sweep is the best option… and you can always photograph unwanted pieces and sell them on eBay! If you are keeping furniture and the upholstery is nearly new, again find a similar sample, or something similar, for your colour board.

Finally, look at the walls. In general, changing the wall colour will be the basis of your new scheme, but if you have a very special wallcovering that you need to retain you will need to include a sample – or something similar – on your colour board.

The right colour scheme...

My advice to anyone when choosing a colour scheme is to play down the colour palette to begin with – you can always add stronger colours as the scheme progresses. It might be fun at first to have a lime green wall and purple rugs scattered around, but six months down the line you will probably wish you had been a tiny bit more reserved in your colour choices! It really is best to go for more muted tones. I don't mean beige, beige and more beige; perhaps try grey for a change – most colours work well with it. I created a lovely scheme with smoky blue for curtains and bed covers, walls two tones lighter and paintwork in a soft stone colour. Add a rug in the same colours plus a muted pink thread running through the design, and it all looked dreamy.

If you are starting from scratch, choose neutral colours for the basics such as carpets and walls and a deeper tone for curtains and upholstery. Brighter items, such as cushions, can then be added later for emphasis.

Making a colour board

The basis for creating any new colour scheme is a colour board. This doesn't have to be anything fancy, simply a board with samples of all the major items in the room, in the correct colours and approximately the right proportions in relation to each other. If you can't include samples of the actual carpet or wallcovering, something similar in the same colour and tone will do. You can usually get small cuttings of fabric from suppliers before buying. When you have made your board, stand back and judge the overall effect. You are looking to achieve a generally muted effect, with perhaps just one or two stronger items to lift the scheme and prevent it being boring. Try to judge the colour board in the actual room – different lighting conditions can make quite a difference.

Existing decor

If you are moving into a new house or flat and the walls are newly painted they will probably be white. Builders must buy cheap white paint in huge 5-litre tins and they seem to slap it on everywhere – but at least this is better than ten years ago when everything was painted magnolia!

If you have a low budget you may decide to save money by 'living' with the existing wall colour but personally I think this is false economy. It doesn't take very long or cost much to repaint walls, then at least you are starting with the right base colour. Perhaps just use a neutral colour to start with – don't try to be too clever.

If your upholstery doesn't work with your new wall colours then throw a linen cover or rug over it, until you can afford to change or reupholster it. Otherwise don't tie yourself down with old baggage – move on. No, you can't alter those old curtains to fit your new windows: nothing looks worse than curtains that have been let down or that don't meet in the middle. Manage without curtains for a while until you have the money to do things properly. You can always hang a wonderful coloured shawl at the bedroom window temporarily – and you might end up by preferring it like that anyway.

The right style of curtains or blinds

It's important to consider the shape, size and function of your window before you decide on the style of curtain or blind to use. Below are a few window styles and some basic guidelines to bear in mind – there are many more sizes and shapes to consider, but if you use this as a rough guide you won't go far wrong.

Basic window

- ▶ A pair of simple curtains on a pole
- ▶ Short or café-style curtains
- ▶ A simple blind so as not to overpower the window

Recessed window

- ▶ Blinds inside the recess should be in translucent fabrics
- ▶ Pole or pelmet fixed on the outside of the recess – but only if there is enough space either side of the window to stack curtains when in the open position
- ▶ Short curtains on a swing-arm bracket

Cottage style

- ▶ Long or short curtains on a pole, but clearing the window frame to let in the maximum light
- ▶ Blinds should be fixed clear of the window frame to allow maximum light

Tips

Never put short curtains on a Georgian window – in fact I don't really like to use short curtains anywhere, unless it is absolutely necessary.

For some ideas on how to treat difficult windows, see Chapter 6.

to suit the window

Dormer window

▶ Portière panels
▶ Blinds fixed as high as possible
▶ Short curtains on a swing-arm bracket

Georgian window

▶ Long, elegant curtains on a pole or with a pelmet
▶ Valances of any kind
▶ Be creative – everything looks good with Georgian windows

Georgian arched window

▶ If you want to emphasise the shape, see page 166 for ideas
▶ Pole fixed above the arch – make sure it is fixed high enough and the curtains can 'stack' out of the way so as not to lose the beautiful shape

Bay windows

▶ A covered lathe (concealed tracking) with long curtains. Can be 2 curtains (one either end), or 3 (one in the middle), or 4 curtains – it depends on the size of the window and the tracking combination
▶ When a bay window is small or you don't want to lose any light, have curtains on a pole across the bay, ignoring its shape completely
▶ Blinds and dress curtains
▶ Blinds only

Basic glazed door shapes

Before you consider curtains for doorways, check that the door does not open inwards or the curtains will get in the way whenever you try to open it. You can, of course, have curtains in this situation but the pole or tracking will have to be fixed well above the doorway and when open the curtains must stack back out of the way on either side, so they are completely clear of the opening door.

Half-glazed Georgian-style door

▶ Curtains must be clear when opening door
▶ Avoid fixing a blind to this kind of door. It is rarely successful – if you really have no alternative then maybe a Roman blind might be the best choice
▶ A good solution would be to have sandblasted glass put into the door

Patio doors

▶ Again, make sure the curtains clear the doorway completely
▶ NEVER have blinds on patio doors
▶ In this situation consider having one big curtain pulling to one side – but you must have the space at the side of the door to 'stack' the big curtain

French doors with side windows

▶ As always, check curtains are clear of the opening of the two central doors – but in this case you can have curtains partly over the side windows, since they do not open

▶ Be sure that your pole or tracking is heavy enough, especially if your fabric is thick, as this kind of door/window has a wide span

▶ Your pole will need a centre bracket for this width

French doors in a bay

▶ There are some very nice steel poles that can be shaped to your bay window (see page 33)

▶ The problem with windows/doors like this is that the bay shape means there is not always enough room to 'stack' the curtains at each side – in this case you could stack them partly over the two fixed windows

Choosing a curtain or blind design

Once you have decided on your plan and have a clear picture in your head of what kind of look you want to achieve then you can select your curtain design and fabric. Give yourself a loose budget, as if you start off with no budget in mind you will so often find the costs spiral out of control and inexpensive fabrics are not so easy to track down these days, unless you stick with cottons from India maybe. Next, look at the shape of your window, as not all kinds of curtains or blinds work for every window. There is a section in this book to guide you through this. Try to follow these basic rules and it will help you to make the right choice of design for the window as well as for the room.

North-facing windows

If the room faces north, it will generally be fairly dark. Avoid blinds that have to be fitted in the window recess, so covering the top part of the window all the time. Definitely don't have a design that needs pelmets or swags and tails, as these will cut out even more of the natural light.

Windows with radiators

Radiators are frequently placed under the windows. This rules out long curtains as you will lose too much heat. You can avoid this by having long dress curtains and then functional blinds that will allow the radiator to do its job properly.

Tall ceilings and big windows

When the windows are big and tall you have so much more scope – choose a flamboyant print in electric colours or just go for simple translucent neutral-coloured blinds to let in as much light as possible. The problem with big windows, of course, is that you need a lot of fabric and that means lots of money – but you can cheat and use a simple calico and add ribbons on the hem. Or put insets of lace and perhaps dye the calico and the lace.

Low ceilings and big windows

Use a striped fabric to create the illusion of ceiling height. Some windows are not very tall but extremely wide, and then I suggest you use the whole wall – hang the curtains from the ceiling and use the entire wall at the side of the windows to stack the curtains back.

Low ceilings and small windows

Curtains for small windows, generally found in country cottages or in attic rooms, should be kept simple. Fabrics should be plain or small prints in delicate colours – nothing too dark or too bright. I suggest you have a voile curtain with a roller blind behind it to pull down at night. I dislike short curtains but sometimes it is unavoidable – if you have to have them I think they are better just lined but not interlined as then they look short AND chunky!

Open or loft-style rooms

This is a good time to experiment – try using large prints, the bolder the better, or you can play it down by choosing neutral-coloured blinds and then cover with vast amounts of voile. Put the voile curtains on electric tracking so you can sweep them dramatically right back to take advantage of a spectacular view. My preference is to use panels on electric tracking. There are many designs for panels in this book, and when you have very tall, wide windows, using panels with tracking generally turns out to be a good solution.

Fabric characteristics...

I used to think that the more you paid for a fabric the better it would be, but there are so many fantastic ones on the market, some ridiculously cheap and others that are beyond most people's budgets, I think that your best bet is to go for something that you really like regardless of the cost – and if it's expensive cut down on something else.

If the windows are small steer clear of heavy fabric, as you will block out too much light. Don't choose thin fabric and try to put in blackout lining, as the curtains won't fall properly. All fabrics will fade if exposed to direct sunlight, so in hotter countries or sunny spots consider shutters or voile curtains. However, basically most fabrics can be adapted to suit the designs in this book – and if you are not sure ask your interior decorator or fabric shop for advice.

Wools and wool mixes

You have a huge range of woollen fabrics, from the soft pastel shades of fine wool and basic flannels, to chunky tweeds. All make up really well and are best in very simple styles. Simple style curtains made in knobbly tweed look marvellous in a big country house. There are plenty of wool tartans around, if you own a Scottish castle – and softer checks in heather mixtures, which are easy to live with and give a comfortable, warm feel to a barn or farmhouse.

Linen and natural weaves

I love all natural weaves, especially linen, which I like to wear whatever the weather. It looks wonderful when used as curtaining or for blinds – it does generally look crumpled and relaxed, but that is what I like about it. Looks best, as far as I am concerned, when used unlined since it does hang so well. If you have chosen a style of curtains or blinds with pin tucks, saddle-stitching or horizontal pleats then this is the fabric to use, as it goes together like a dream.

There are many wonderful colours to choose from. For some time I liked the natural string colour, but now I am experimenting and have come up with a lovely soft coloured pallete with muted blues, lilac and greys and it looks lovely... so I may get out of my beige rut and be a bit more adventurous!

Tips

Always use thread to match the composition of your curtain.

When buying fabric, check the laundering instructions on the fabric bolt.

Some natural weaves have slubs as part of their composition. These are not faults, but if they are very obvious be aware of where they will fall when measuring and cutting.

Cotton

Most cotton fabrics are relatively inexpensive, which is why they are so popular, I suppose. The only time I use it is for curtains or blinds in a kitchen or bathroom since it can be machine washed. Be careful to have a washable lining if the curtains are lined. Children's bedroom curtains are also best in cotton for the same reason. If you use a blackout lining (one of the new soft ones on the market, not the thick smelly rubber kind) and your curtains are machine made, then this is an ideal hardwearing fabric.

Tips

Depending on how cotton is finished it can have a matte or a shiny texture. These special finishes are often removed when the fabric is washed..

Shiny fabrics reflect light, making the room appear bigger. Matte fabrics absorb light, making the room appear smaller.

Check the fabric width – narrow widths will mean you need more lengths of fabric to create your curtains, so what appears to be an inexpensive fabric can end up costing more in the long run.

Velvet

When I think of velvet I think of cinema seats or formal swags
and tails in a theatre, but there are some really nice velvets
around at present – look for panné velvet and you will find a
soft floppy fabric that hangs beautifully when made into curtains.
Don't use it for blinds. There are lots of cut velvets around and
these have a younger feel to them. Another favourite is Paisley
printed velvet. Still, if you want formal curtains, then velvet is still
the best fabric. It can look special when you overload the
curtains with trimmings, such as bullion fringe mixed with
embroidered wide ribbons. You must line velvet, but if it is heavy
you can miss out the interlining. Look for chenille, which is nicer
than velvet to my mind.

Tips

When using several lengths of fabric with a pile, make
sure the pile runs in the same direction on each piece,
or they will look as if they are different colours.

Do not cut off selvedges when working with velvet, as it
frays very badly.

Silks

This is my favourite fabric. As a dress designer in the sixties I
used it for everything – it was a great luxury then but now it
can be found to suit everyone's pocket. I have used it for
palaces and for penthouses and it always looks stunning. There
are so many colours to choose from and such wonderful prints
around. Also, most fabric manufacturers have embroidered silks
now, from India and Japan, which are very popular. When using
silk, make sure there is plenty of fullness in the curtains and let
the fabric fall on the floor – you can spoil the effect if you skimp
on the fabric. Try adding beaded fringing to the leading edge.
Depending on the style, I usually line and interline silk curtains
unless I am going for a particular casual look – when I use
double the amount of fabric. If the type of silk is crumpled and
natural then I often leave out the interlining and sometimes
even the lining.

Tips

To avoid puckered seams when sewing silk, place a layer
of thin tissue paper above and below the seam, then
stitch right through it. You can tear the tissue gently away
when you have finished..

Silk is very strong, but repeated exposure to direct
sunlight will weaken it and eventually cause it to
disintegrate. Line silk curtains if you want to use them in
a sunny window.

Voiles (sheers)

This delicate translucent fabric is very popular – there are some wonderful embroidered voiles to be found and although some of them are very expensive you will find some from India that are priced more realistically. If you are using voile for blinds make sure you have the fabric treated before the blind is made up – most good blind manufacturers will do this. I like to put voile curtains in front of an ordinary roller blind to soften the starkness of the blind and often use Italian stringing to dramatically sweep the curtains to one side on a large window.

Tips

Use lots of fabric when making up voile into curtains, as it looks pathetic when it is too skimpy.

Voile doesn't only have to be used in conjunction with over-curtains – in the right scheme it can look stunning used on its own.

Voiles will not cut out light – use a light-resistant blind behind them.

Dos

These dos are very important, so read this carefully...

1 First of all, spend time deciding on the type of window covering you want.

2 Check that the blind or curtain is suitable for your window shape.

3 Be careful not to block out too much light, for instance by covering the window with a very heavy pelmet.

4 Check if your window faces north, as this will always be dark and you will need to allow as much light as possible into the room.

5 Choose a fabric that goes with the rest of your soft furnishings, as otherwise you will need to change everything to match your window coverings – could be expensive!

6 Measure your window correctly, especially if you are having blinds.

7 When measuring always use a metal retractable tape measure.

8 If you find that the curtains you have chosen still block out too much light, hold them back with a tie-back or hold-back.

9 With certain fabrics you do need to line and interline them to get the best effect, so do spend that extra money on doing this.

10 Do be absolutely sure you are happy with your choice of fabric, especially if it is bright and bold – you will have to live with this for at least 10 years.

Don't skip this list – it is important!

1 Never choose a style of window covering that blocks out too much light; it is depressing to live with, especially in winter.

2 When choosing the fabric try to avoid big bold prints in small rooms.

3 If your windows are tall don't even think about short curtains, whatever the reason, as they will look ridiculous. If there is no other way around it – don't have curtains at all!

4 Don't make the mistake of having curtains over a window that opens inwards – the treatment has to clear the opening window.

5 If you are having a valance or pelmet with the curtains don't make them too shallow, as this is a common mistake. Be sure you look at the window and the length of the curtains before making the final choice – be bold with your decision.

6 If you try to put light-resistant lining in a flimsy fabric you will have a disaster on your hands, so avoid this at all costs. Use a roller blind behind the curtains instead.

7 Don't skimp on buying less fabric by ignoring the pattern matching – you will regret this every time you close your curtains or blinds.

8 Never make the curtains too short as you will spoil the whole effect. Curtains should just 'break' on the floor or, in certain styles, even crumple onto the floor in a puddle.

9 Don't make the mistake of putting a blind in a recessed window as it will block out the light. Always put the blind on the wall above the recess.

10 Be careful when using trimmings on curtains or blinds – sometimes you can 'over trim.' If you have a plain fabric it can be fun to overdo things but with printed fabrics generally less is more.

2

Essentials

Introduction to essentials...

Choosing your curtain system...
In some cases there will be few options when it comes to choosing the type of curtains you want and what support system to have, but in others the possibilities are endless. Use this section to work out what will be the best choice in any given scenario.

Poles

Curtain poles are almost invariably fitted above the window recess, and they are designed to be on show. They are usually made of either wood or metal, but there is a wide range of finishes available in both types. The pole itself is generally rather plain, as the curtain has to slide along it, but decorative finials and the selection of curtain suspension system – hooks, rings, rope, eyelets – can make the design possibilities almost endless.

Poles can be used in both a traditional and a modern interior – there are design styles for both – and can be a major feature of the curtain design or just a background support system. When choosing your style of pole, be guided by the style of the curtain design itself.

Tracks

In general, tracks are concealed – they are intended to be purely a support system for the curtain and a means to enable them to be drawn. Heavy-duty tracks are made from metal, the lighter weight types are plastic. Make sure you have a suitable type, as curtains can be surprisingly heavy.

Some tracks are corded, which means that they have a system of pulleys and cords threaded up within the track and coming down at one side that allow the curtain to be drawn open and closed by pulling on a cord, rather than tugging the curtain itself. Some of these corded systems are even motorized – essential for very large and heavy curtains, such as stage or cinema curtaining.

Covered lathes

A covered lathe is a flat length of wood that is covered in fabric and fixed to the front of a curtain track to conceal the track itself and its workings. It should be wide enough to hide the track, but does not need to be as deep nor as dressy as a pelmet or a valance. They are only used when a pelmet or valance is not suitable for some reason – either because of the type of window or door, or because the style of curtain does not need a dressy heading.

Covered lathes are not required on dress curtains that meet in the centre to totally cover the track, but are a nice touch on curtains that do draw, as they hide the expanse of track between the two curtains when they are open.

Panel glides

In a panel glide system, the panels hang flat without any fullness and glide as a unit over the window. If the opening size requires more than one panel, the panels can be staggered on the track so they stack up to just one panel width at the side. There is generally a limit of about ten metres to the maximum opening width that can be accommodated, while the width of each individual panel is dictated by the width of the fabric available.

Like curtains, panels can be operated by hand – usually by means of a draw rod – with a cording system or by a motor. Panels are a great way to show off a spectacular fabric, as the details of the design are not lost within many folds of fabric.

Bay windows

Bay windows are the focal point of any room, as they are often large and let in the light, giving a great feeling of space. When you have a bay window in a room you will generally find there is another straight window in the room that should have the same style and fabric. A bay window can have two to six curtains depending on the size of the window. If there is a window seat in the bay it would be better to have functional Roman blinds and have dress curtains either side.

Curtain fittings

The heading chosen for a curtain will, to some extent, dictate what sort of fittings can be used. Simple gathered headings only need standard-size curtain hooks, but some of the more complex, tall headings need special longer hooks that will hold the weight of the heading upright and not allow it to droop.

Curtain rings come in a range of types and finishes to match the pole they are to be teamed with. Some rings are designed to be used with curtain hooks, others have clips on the base that just clip onto the curtain.

Tabs and ties are generally made in the same fabric as the curtain, but can be made in a contrast colour or replaced with ribbon or rope for a different look. Browse through the heading pages in this chapter to see a host of different ideas.

Valances

Valances are soft and made of fabric and have a heading the same as a curtain. In many ways they are a curtain in miniature, but are not intended to draw – instead they stay fixed in place to hide the curtain fixings and the top of the curtain.

If a curtain is to have a valance the curtain itself should have a simple heading, since this will be concealed – any more complex heading to complete the design should be used on the valance. Although valances are generally not used with a pelmet, this is by no means a rule – some more elaborate designs will use both.

Pelmets

A pelmet is usually a solid three-dimensional box, with a front and a return at either side, that is fixed above the window recess to cover the top of the curtain and all its fixings. In some cases the pelmet may be a flat board that is fixed across the window recess, if the curtains are hung within the recess and not face-fixed.

Pelmets can be covered in fabric to co-ordinate with the curtains, and they can be trimmed in the same way and with the same materials as the curtains. They can also be carved, polished or painted wood, or even finished to match the walls of the room.

Traditional poles and finials

There are some amazing carved poles and finials to be found, whatever the period of your house – from Victorian and Art Deco to Georgian. Choose a pole the correct thickness for the weight of your curtains, and remember that a pole that is too thin looks odd with long curtains; try to get the right balance.

If you choose a Candy Twist pole you will find the rings don't slide easily over the twist parts, so perhaps use this pole for dress curtains.

Your poles and finials can generally be stained to any colour or even painted to tie in with your colour scheme. If you are using wooden hold-backs, then don't forget to stain or paint them the same colour as the pole and finials.

 Ball

 Provençal style

 Reeded finial and pole

 Fluted ball

 Antique brass finial and pole

 Wooden hand-carved finial

 Trumpet finial in two colours of wood

 Art Deco

 Gilded wooden finial and pole

 Inverted rib and cage

 Early Victorian-style 'spinning top'

 Leaf and acorn

 Minaret candy twist pole

 Victorian scroll

 Coronet with decorative pole

 Ottoman

Contemporary poles and finials

Brushed steel poles suit the sleek lines of minimalist curtains, especially in loft-style apartments. There are plenty of unusual shapes to choose from, but I have selected a few that I use constantly. I like to keep the pole and finial as plain as possible so as not to distract from the curtain design or the fabric – the simpler the better as far as I am concerned. There are double poles on the market now and this gives a much cleaner look when you have a voile (sheer) curtain behind the main

curtain, since you don't have to have tracking behind the pole. I use the black iron poles for country houses as they blend in beautifully with rustic interiors.

NOTE: If the pole is longer than 3m (10ft) you will need a centre bracket. Buy a good-quality metal pole then it won't rust. Otherwise, varnish a cheaper one with a yacht varnish to keep it from rusting.

 Steel spire

 Wooden 'bamboo' ball

 Steel ribbon ball

 Iron button

 Iron ball

 Iron knot

 Cage and ball

 Shepherd's crook

 Roped ball

 Steel pole with raised steel bands

 Steel pole with shaped steel finial

 Steel corkscrew

 Steel rib

 Metal ball

 Steel pole with corded finial

 Polished nickel finial and pole

Modern tracking systems

There are quite a few very good modern tracking systems to be found on the market these days. A selection of the best types are shown here. Also some manufacturers have finally sorted out a solution to the drama of having a curtain pole in a bay window – and about time too.

1

Stainless steel roller line pole. Can also be used for bay windows.

2

Stainless steel flat pole system – can be bent to form a return.

3

Tension wire system used from wall to wall. You can now have a 'long span' wire (ask your manufacturer for a leaflet on this).

4

Stainless steel pole. Can be used with tension wire for second curtain.

5

Steel or iron arm used for recessed windows or room dividers.

6

Various metal spiral rings – use for curtains with eyelet hole headings.

Tips

Be warned when using any of these systems – always read the manufacturer's instructions carefully.

Wire tracking can be used to hang lightweight curtains from wall to wall, within reason of course (see diagram 3).

Wire tracking is also useful when hanging curtains in a recessed window.

When ordering poles for a bay window always be sure the diagram is correct (see page 33).

Double poles are wonderful – now you can have a lightweight voile curtain behind your main ones without two lots of tracking or a pole combined with tracking, which can be very messy.

Steel or iron arms are useful in dormer windows or cottage windows that are recessed.

Steel poles for bay windows

ALWAYS CHECK AND DOUBLE CHECK your diagram and dimensions before ordering these poles, as they cannot be altered once they are made and they are quite expensive.

Modern stainless steel poles can be made to fit any bay or difficult window. They are available in double poles too, which is wonderful for voiles and curtains at the same window.

There is only one drawback with these poles – you cannot have your curtains on pull cords (either manual or electric) so the curtains must be opened and closed by hand.

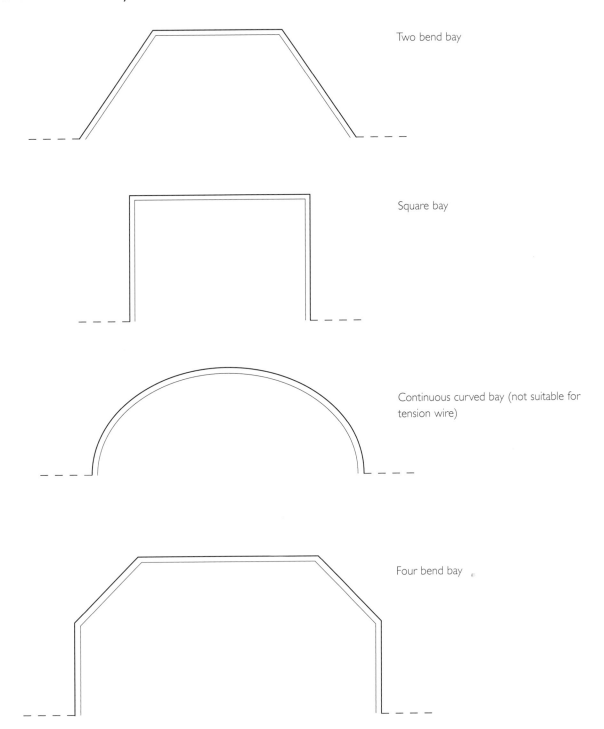

Two bend bay

Square bay

Continuous curved bay (not suitable for tension wire)

Four bend bay

Panel glide system

This is a relatively new system and it brings a totally new dimension to a room. Panels work really well in the home as well as in an office.

The tracking is fixed onto the ceiling or onto the wall and the panels hang straight down, without any fullness like a curtain. They are a wonderful way to show off a large print, which would normally be lost in the folds of a curtain.

The panel glide is available as either hand, cord or electrically operated – the hand-operated ones are pulled with an aluminium draw rod. When the panels are connected, which is required for hand as well as electrically operated types, the leading panel pulls the other panels along in sequence.

Panels can be specified to most reasonable sizes but anything over 6m (19ft) wide would depend on the weight of the fabric and the manufacturer you are using. The maximum length is generally 10m (32ft).

The panel fold is a motorized system, which can be operated by a fixed wall switch or even remote control. Panel folds are suitable for applications up to 5m (16ft) wide and 3m (10ft) drop. This type of panel can be hung rather closer to the ceiling than the sliding panel system.

Here are a few sketches of panels, which show how versatile the panels are.

Two panels can be operated in the same way as curtains or can open to one side only.

A single panel in translucent fabric that can close either way.

Panels can be used as 'doors' in front of a wardrobe or messy area like a child's toy cupboard.

Panels are best if the windows are very wide.

Basic curtain headings

Regis or Pencil pleat

Unstructured

Triple pinch pleat or French pleat

Goblet or Tulip

Unstructured with stand

Tab

Ties

Ties with rope

Eyelet

Eyelet with rope

Basic curtain headings

Soft tuck on rings

Clips on runner

Pinch pleat unstructured

Loops

Rope

Floppy heading

Pocket/rod heading

Smocking

Soft box pleat

Inverted pleat

Valances

Regis or Pencil pleat

Pencil pleat with dropped sides

Pinch pleat

Goblet

Gathered

Tab

Tie

Regis or Pencil pleat with trim

Slotted heading with dropped sides

Draped

Pelmets

Fabric-covered pelmet with shaped base and contrast border

Fabric-covered pelmet with scalloped base and contrast border

Pelmet with Russian braid trim

Plain pelmet with braid and frogging detail

Shaped pelmet trimmed with tasselled fringing

Chevron pelmet with two co-ordinating fabrics

Fabric-covered pelmet with braid trim

Fabric-covered pelmet cut-out design

Fabric-covered pelmet with raised saddle-stitched lattice

Fabric-covered pelmet with Russian braid and button detailing

43

Hard carved pelmets

Simple pelmet with cornice and Greek key design

Wooden pelmet with cornice and fretwork scroll

Elaborate pelmet with egg and dart cornice and shaped base

Cornice pelmet with carved roses

Modern corniced pelmet with scalloped edge

Basketwork coronet with swags of roses and ribbons

Coronet, used above a bed

Hard carved pelmets and fretwork

Simple modern pelmet with central cut-out detail

Plain pelmet with repeated chevron cut-out detail

Wallpaper-covered pelmet with scalloped cut-out base

Simple fretwork pelmet

Elaborate fretwork pelmet

Wooden pelmet with repeating fretwork design

3

Finishing Touches

Introduction to finishing touches...

Adding that final touch...
Sometimes a fairly plain curtain design can be transformed, just by adding that one, perfect trim or the ideal tie-back. This chapter is designed to give you some ideas on how you can make your curtains look just that little bit more special.

Braids and ribbons

Braids and ribbons are the simplest and easiest trim you can add to a curtain design, but the effects you can achieve are stunning. Braids come in all designs, colours and styles, so you are sure to find the perfect one for your curtain. Russian braid is so versatile and easy to form into interesting shapes – the possibilities are almost endless!

Ropes and tassels

Ropes were traditionally often used as an extra design feature on curtains with swags and tails, but now they can be a decorative detail in themselves. Trim manufacturers make a standard range of ropes – many co-ordinated with matching tassels and trims – but can also make up colourways to order.

Tassels can be added alone or as the finishing touch to a length of rope. Again, they come in standard colourways to match other trims, or can be made up in special colours to match your fabric exactly.

Fringe and beaded trims

Fringing is created by weaving braid so that it has loops of yarn hanging downward from the base, and the lengths of fringe can be left in loops or sometimes trimmed into single strands. Bullion fringe has uncut loops twisted together to look like single strands, and is a particularly heavy, traditional type of fringe.

Beaded trims have beads or crystals that are either suspended from lengths of ribbon trim or threaded onto the loops of a fringed braid. This type of trim is ideal to add a touch of sparkle at the window.

Tie-backs and hold-backs

Tie-backs are lengths of fabric or rope that tie the curtain back against the wall and away from the window opening when they are not in use. They can be trimmed to match the curtain, and this chapter gives you plenty of ideas.

Hold-backs are solid metal or wood knobs or hooks that are fixed to the wall. When the curtain is drawn back it can be caught behind the hold-back to hold it in position. Both tie-backs and hold-backs can be used to keep dress curtains permanently in place.

Plain and trimmed

Adding a luxurious trimming like this can transform plain curtains.

Emphasize the unusual shape of this design with a simple beaded fringe.

Trimmings

 Decorative braid

 Picot ribbon with beaded edge

 Grosgrain braid

 Single edged picot

 Delicate glass beaded fringe

 Pleated ribbon braid

 Picot beaded fringe

 Swirl motif on grosgrain ribbon

 Novelty glass beaded fringe

 Striped braid

 Crystal and silk beaded fringe

 Jacquard border

 Venetian-style beaded fringe

Gimp

 Picot ribbon

 Rope

 Flanged rope

 Looped fan edge

 Twisted loop fringe

 Fan edge

 Looped fan edge with tassels

 Onion tassel fringe

 Neo-classical hanger fringe

 Bullion fringe with bead hangers

 Bullion fringe

 Tufted fringe

 Striped braid with knotted pom-poms

Finishing Touches

51

Trimmings

Bow braid woven tape

Tufted braid in fine hand-woven yarns

Glass-beaded fringe

Pear-drop beaded fringe on gimp

Shell chip fringe

Pebble bead fringe

Lozenge fringe

Lantern hanger fringe

18th-century tassel fringe

Butterfly beaded fringe

Bauble hanger fringe

Novelty hanging ropes used as decoration on curtains or accessories

A kind of 'key tassel' with a bauble instead of a tassel

A quilted hem on the curtain and throw, plus a wonderful looped trim on the leading edge of the curtain.

By adding trimmings to your other soft furnishings, as shown here, you add a touch of professionalism.

Trimmings

A contemporary collection of simple woven braids and fringes, all combining a wrapped technique and style. The two tie-backs offer a less formal design with a more modern approach.

Flanged rope

Double cut fringe

Cut fringe

Unusual tie-backs

Picot ribbon with covered lozenges

Picot ribbon with lozenge-style covered shape

Elegance and glamour – a combination of crystal and glass trimmings for an opulent interior. Swarovski crystals delicately woven into silk braid headings and hand-twisted cords.

Crystal drop fringe

Crystal icicle fringe

Crystallia tie-back

Icicle hangers

Murano glass lantern fringe

Murano glass tie-backs

Bead and crystal hangers

55

Beaded trimmings

This Roman blind and dressed curtain are both edged
with a stunning crystal trim.

Unstructured curtain with beaded trim.

Two-tiered curtains with beaded fringe.

One-sided curtain with delicate crystal trimmings.

Printed voile with looped beading on the hem.

Ribbons and braids

Hessian ribbons machined onto the fabric in a simple grid.

Fringed heavy wool curtains with a wide Jacquard ribbon border.

A simple picot ribbon machined along the leading edge and forming a square 'knot' design in the bottom corner. The heading ties are the same ribbon.

Sewing picot ribbons on vertically visually adds height to the curtains.

Tasselled trimmings

Plain curtains with a
gathered valance...

... are transformed by adding tassel fringing to the
valance and rope to the leading edges of the curtain.

Accentuate the shape of this design by adding unusual fringing.

Valance with a slotted heading and edged with tassels, over dressed curtains and an Italian-strung curtain.

Mixing trimmings

To achieve a unique look, try using wide ribbon as a base and adding various other trimmings.

Woven braid, rope and beaded fringe.

Rope, woven ribbon and buttons on picot.

Grosgrain ribbon, picot ribbon and rope.

Rope, Jacquard ribbon and tassel fringe.

Tie-backs

Cord, loop and beaded tie-backs offer a less formal
alternative to the formal tassel tie-back. Most trimming
ranges include these, to co-ordinate with the other
trimmings.

Contemporary tie-backs

Contemporary bauble tie-backs – covered wooden moulds are an alternative to tassel tie-backs.

Wrapped and bound tassel tie-backs in a contemporary style.

Elegant tassel decorations – crystal, bead and lozenge designs.

Traditional tie-backs

Traditional decorative tie-backs with beaded and tassel hangers.

Casual, less formal tie-backs.

Tie-backs influenced by historical designs.

Fabric tie-backs

Simple crescent

Scalloped edge

Crescent with bias-cut frill

Casual knotted crescent

Tied crescent

Crescent with pleated frill

Bias-cut crescent

Plaited fabric

Plain and simple band

Band trimmed with beaded fringe

Hold-backs

These 'hold-backs' are designed to neatly hold back the curtain to let in more light.

'Ombres' or 'embraces' gather up the curtain.

Modern metal swing-arm hold-backs, used for voile or sheer curtains.

4

Basic Headings

Introduction to basic headings...

Choosing a heading...
The heading you choose for your curtain will often set the style for the whole design, so it's worth taking some time to get it right. Here we look at the different headings and how to achieve them, and on the following pages you will see the headings in action on a curtain, valance or pelmet.

Pencil pleat

Regis heading, also sometimes called a pencil pleat heading. A regis heading tape is sewn on near the top of the curtains and the strings on the tape are pulled to form a neat row of single pencil pleats right across the top.

Triple pinch pleat

The triple pinch pleat is also sometimes called the French pleat. It can be made using heading tape but for the best effect use curtain buckram between the layers at the top of the curtain. Pockets are formed on the face of the curtain and are then pinched together to form either double or triple pleats.

Floppy

Cut the curtain longer, adding double the amount you want the curtain to flop over into a frill at the top, plus another 2.5cm (1in) to go under the tape. Turn over the fabric and the lining to the back of the curtain and sew on a narrow heading tape to cover the raw edge. Pull the strings to the required width, then turn over the flop.

Goblet

This heading is sometimes called a tulip heading. Like the pinch pleat, it can be done with a heading tape but is best formed in the same way as described for pinch pleats. The tops are then opened up to form a goblet, with wadding or a separate curl of buckram inserted to maintain the goblet shape.

Slotted

The slotted heading is also sometimes called a pocket heading or in US a rod pocket. This is a slot or pocket formed across the top of the curtain, sometimes with an upstand for a more decorative effect. The slot should be a bit bigger than the pole so that the curtain slides onto it easily.

Inverted pleat

This is a very casual heading, a simple inverted pleat caught with stitches at the top of the curtain to hold the pleat in place. It can have buckram for a stiff top but I prefer to keep it soft and less formal.

Box pleat

A square pleat at intervals across the heading. Work out how many box pleats you need for the width of each curtain. Make sure you allow the same amount of fabric under the pleat or the curtain will not fall correctly. Pin the pleats in place and gently press the top only. Machine or hand sew the pleat across the base. For a more formal heading use buckram. This heading can only be used for static curtains, as they will not draw back from the window.

Tab

The tabs are made out of strips of fabric, looped over with the raw ends placed between the curtain and the lining at the top and sewn in place. The tabs should be bigger than the pole so that they slide along to open and close easily.

Unstructured

The unstructured heading is a dainty heading, which is best for thin delicate fabrics such as voile or lawn. Use a heading tape that is sewn onto the top of the curtain; when the strings are pulled it gathers into narrow informal pleats.

Pinch pleat unstructured

Just take a small pinch of fabric and sew to a ring at equal intervals along the top of the curtain, then thread the rings onto a pole. No buckram – keep this very soft.

Eyelet

For people sewing at home, the best way to achieve eyelets is to use heading tape stitched in place, then cut the holes by hand and clip the eyelets together from either side of the hole. The alternative is to hire or buy a rather expensive manual hole punch or eyelet machine. Alternatively, you might find a workroom who can punch the eyelets in for you for a small charge.

When the eyelets are in place, they are then simply threaded onto a pole, or rope is looped through each and over the pole in between.

Clip

The clips are attached to the bottom of the rings that slide onto the curtain pole, or to a runner system. The top of the curtain should have some thickness so that the clip has something to fix to – make sure your fabric is not too heavy as often clips will not take much weight. They are great for sheers and lightweight, unlined cottons.

Ties

These are similar to tabs, but the ties are two separate strips of fabric that just tie over the top of the pole. Instead of fabric ties you can use short lengths of rope stitched to the top of the curtain at intervals.

Basic headings

One-sided Italian-strung curtain with huge looped trimming.

Pencil

Insets of fabric are edged with a simple tassel trim.

Short curtains should only be used when there is no alternative.

A one-sided curtain is a great solution for a deeply recessed window.

Basic headings

A triple pleat heading adds interest to the simple lines of this curtain.

Use a contrast lining, pulled back and hooked onto the tie-backs.

Emphasize the triple pinch pleats with tiny tassels at the base of each set.

Pinch pleated

Appliqué on the leading edge of the curtain adds a touch of drama.

This classic design has a goblet-pleated valance and the curtains are draped softly over hold-backs.

Italian-strung curtains are ideal for a very formal setting. Ropes and tassels add extra interest.

Basic headings

A simple, classic goblet heading.

Goblet

Large square buttons at the base of each goblet match the colour of the contrast trim on the leading edge and hem of the curtains.

Heavy bullion fringing works best on a heavyweight fabric, such as wool tweed.

Basic
Headings

Two-tone rope looks spectacular along the leading edge of the curtains and knotted under the goblets.

Basic headings

A slotted heading is ideal to dress a big window in a
simple way. Add extra interest with an attractive hold-
back.

Slotted/pocket

A double curtain on a double rail – and the
over-curtain is lined in the same contrast fabric used for
the under-curtain.

This shaped dress curtain frames the window.
The blind behind it is functional.

The long dress curtains are not intended to close. The
voile café curtain is trimmed with bands of matching
ribbon.

Basic headings

Here, the contrast border is
repeated along the bottom edge of
the valance and enhanced with an
appliqué design at the centre of
the window.

A wide Jacquard ribbon bordering
the leading edge and deep fringing
on the hem give a different look.

Inverted pleat

A wide contrast border all around the edges creates a dramatic outline.

Silk curtains are given an extra touch of luxury with a deep frilled border.

The edge of this Italian-strung portière curtain is highlighted with wide braid.

Basic headings

Basic
Headings

Basic plain tab curtains are simple and elegant.

A deep frill in matching or contrasting fabric creates interest at the base of the curtain.

Three-tiered frill cut on the bias for a soft, romantic look.

Buttoned tabs in the same dramatic contrast fabric used for the borders of this two-tier curtain.

Hessian tabs with matching tassels add extra emphasis to the heading.

Basic headings

Inset contrast bands set on the diagonal for extra flair. Bias-cut fabric hangs beautifully.

Large bold prints need large bold details – such as this deep frill.

Tab

A simple design is given wow-factor by the triangular over-hanging with tassels and a deep bullion fringe at the hem.

Double contrasting bands at the hem are echoed by the alternating tabs at the heading.

Box pleated and buttoned tabs give a smart tailored look.

Jute fringing is matched with jute tabs for a fully co-ordinated design.

Basic headings

The casual crumpled look of an unstructured heading looks great in linen.

Unstructured

Double curtain, with a tiny check pattern on the under-curtain that is echoed in the 'Robin Hood' turnovers at the top of the over-curtain.

A valance cut on the bias hangs in soft folds that complement the unstructured look.

The handkerchief points of the skirt are emphasized by the contrast border, which is repeated along the leading edge of the curtain. Appliqué adds extra style.

A two-tiered curtain with wide contrast bands will make a very tall window look shorter.

Basic headings

Eyelet curtains are very practical across alcove openings, creating an eye-catching panel of colour when closed.

Double-sided curtains are hooked back to reveal the contrast lining. Here they hide unsightly computer equipment.

Eyelet

Two-tone fabric in a chequerboard pattern is set off with contrast saddle stitching.

For a truly rustic look, nothing can beat a sack cloth curtain.

Smart Russian braid on the leading edge and along the base of the valance evokes a military look.

Canvas curtains with lacing across the centre give a nautical feel.

Basic headings

Absolutely no sewing required – just clip a lightweight
rug or blanket onto a pole.

Clip

One-sided curtains are ideal for a portière. Emphasize the curve of the edge with fringing.

A simple panel curtain clipped to a pole and pinned back at the centre.

Black studs on box pleats echo the colour of the iron pole. The curtains are pulled back and tied to reveal the stylish checked lining.

Basic headings

Tie-on headings and a deep frill on silk curtains give a
romantic look suitable for a bedroom.

Heavily contrasting bands are very dramatic and the horizontal lines make a narrow window look wider.

A variation with zigzag bands instead of straight lines, making the curtains look long and elegant.

Diagonal lines of crystal trimmings add style and sparkle.

Using beaded string to tie the curtain to the pole creates an informal feel.

Basic headings

The dark and heavy pole is balanced by the wide
contrast band at the base of the valance, and the
matching square buttons at the base of each triple
pleat.

Soft valance

An unstructured clip-on valance creates a soft informal look.

The box pleats at the top are attached to the rings with studs. Deep fringing on both hems is made of rough wool.

The deep crystal edging on the top skirt of this double curtain is at eye-level for maximum impact.

Valances

Studded box heading and valance edged with Russian braid.

Contemporary steel pole with tie-on valance.

The wonderful bold print used for the valance is also the curtain lining.

Valances

This valance is cut on the bias so it falls beautifully.

A simple valance made special by using a large cabbage rose print.

Plenty of beaded trim is wonderful for a bedroom.

Unusual spotted valance with a coordinated jet beaded trim.

Valances

A box-pleated heading on this gathered valance. It has
a pretty shape with the drop in the middle as well as at
the sides, and the curtain is lined in matching material.

Valances

Pencil pleat valance with dropped sides, its classic shape emphasized with a double line of Russian braid.

A shaped pencil pleat valance with a bias-cut frill that gently flutes.

Draped valance with a deep bullion fringe.

Valances

Black and white rope trim to match the black and
white colourway of this dramatic spotted fabric. The
rope is added to show off this simple traditional shape.

Valances

A simple gathered heading on this valance with a stand. The valance has over-long droopy sides edged with a pretty looped fringe.

A double pleated valance with droopy sides, heavily trimmed with beads.

Valance co-ordinated with the centre section of a curtain with mixed fabrics, and trimmed with a matching bobble fringe.

Pelmets

A wonderful boldly spotted pelmet – but keep the main curtains plain.

Wide black braid on the pelmet and hem is echoed in the smart black buttons.

Russian braid is really easy to stitch on so you can create your own designs.

The colours of the wide striped pelmet are complemented in the plain curtain and border.

Pelmets

This unusual one-side, double-scallop pelmet is quilted.

Quilted pelmets look best in plain velvet, teamed with soft silk curtains.

Before cutting the fabric for this pelmet, make an accurate paper pattern of the design motif.

Huge flowers make a dramatic statement on this spectacular pelmet – team it with plain curtains.

5

Traditional and Modern Designs

Introduction to styles...

Choosing your style...
Sometimes a fairly plain curtain can be transformed, just by adding that one, perfect trim or the ideal tie-back.

This chapter is designed to give you some ideas on how you can make your curtains look just that little bit more special.

Swags and tails

Swags and tails are an essential feature of many classic curtain styles – the swag is the sweeping drape of fabric across the top of the curtain head, the tail is the end of fabric that hangs down in graceful folds at the side. Even the most simple swag and tails will add a touch of elegance to a curtain design, but there are hundreds of variations on the basic theme, some of them extremely elaborate.

Despite their classical roots, swags and tails have also been incorporated in modern designs – sometimes in quite eyecatching and unusual ways. Although usually a team, swags can be used without tails and tails without swags. Informal swags can be created just by draping lengths of fabric or a beautiful shawl across a curtain pole.

Contemporary

Modern designs tend to use simpler headings than the traditional designs, or to use entirely different ways of supporting the curtain: eyelet holes, rope, ties or tabs, for instance. Modern designs also sometimes combine elements in an unusual way, or use items that would not normally be considered for a window treatment, such as greenery, simple fabric panels or using sheers without an over-curtain.

Although generally less elaborate than traditional curtains, contemporary curtains can still be very elegant and stylish. Dress curtains are not so often part of the design, but a modern design may still include two layers, perhaps with co-ordinating fabrics.

Classic styles

Traditional curtain designs range from simple but well-dressed to extremely elaborate. They don't necessarily need to have swags and tails; they may have a decorative pelmet or a draped valance, or just feature an elegant heading on a beautiful pole, while fringes, ropes and tassels are often part of the design.

It is also common to have more than one layer in a classic design. Since much of the appeal of a traditional design is in the beautiful way it is arranged, dress curtains – which can be left in their place – are often teamed with a secondary window covering that is functional: perhaps an elaborate over-curtain over sheers, or an Italian-strung curtain over some type of blind. The dress or over-curtain should also be fully lined – a single layer of fabric will not hang elegantly.

Bay windows

Bay windows can be hard to design for – do you dress them as one unit, or as separate windows? If the bay has French doors it makes things even more complicated. Much will depend on how deep the bay is, how close its component windows are to each other and whether there is seating.

Both traditional and modern curtain designs will work on a bay – so ultimately the choice of design will depend on the style of the rest of the room. For a range of alternative ideas for a bay, see pages 132 to 137.

Italian stringing

These angled draperies with a straight hem line are a difficult treatment to make successfully. Italian stringing is a method of 'stringing' or 'opening' curtains in which the curtains are fixed at the top, so the only parts that move are the bottoms – these are pulled up by means of a cord or multiple cords attached to the back.

Because the heading is fixed in place, Italian-strung curtains are often the ideal solution for unusual window shapes – particularly if it's the shape of the window head that is the problem. They are also great as dress curtains, since they are not intended to draw.

Sheers/voiles

Sheers have often been treated as unimportant – just there to obscure glass for privacy. However, modern sheers come in such a wide range of colours, designs and prints that they can make a statement all of their own. Sheers are often teamed with dress curtains, but can also be layered alone for a light window style. They are excellent if there is no need for the light to be obscured, as they will allow natural light to filter through.

Dress curtains

A dress curtain is any curtain that is designed for show and not to actually draw across the window. It doesn't necessarily have to be actually fixed in place so it cannot draw – it is just a curtain that is not intended to draw and so its design can be more elaborate. The way it is dressed at the window can also be more elaborate, as it does not have to be returned to position each time it is moved. Dress curtains are usually teamed with an alternative window treatment, either a blind, sheers or a secondary curtain.

Swags and tails

Swags and tails in a highly patterned fabric accentuated
with ropes and tassels complement a simple
unstructured curtain.

A traditional design teamed with a candy twist pole.

A simplified modern version of swags and tails.

Swags and tails combined with a carved pelmet and a one-sided Italian-strung curtain.

Swags and tails used alone are a useful treatment for a round window.

Swags and tails

An elegant design with swags and tails edged with
beading and a patterned voile under-curtain beneath
an unstructured and softly draped over-curtain.

Traditional swags and tails edged with deep fringing.

Use a heavy fabric for this design, teamed with a heavy fringe.

A more modern version of swags and tails, with fabric gathered and draped from an upright finial at each end.

Swags and tails

A classic design in which the bold braid edging
accentuates the curve of the swag and the meandering
folds of the tails.

Triple swags edged with a deep crystal fringe and highlighted with bold rosettes.

Heavy tweed trimmed with wool bullion fringe, ideal for a plain, bold interior.

Dressing a window recess just with swags and tails works well if there is no room for curtains.

Traditional

Carved roses on the pelmet with lots of hanging crystals and crystal trim to the swags.

A very formal design with a deep pelmet, swags and tails that should only be used if the ceilings are high.

Another very formal design but a narrower and less elaborate pelmet means it can be used with lower ceilings.

A pretty carved pelmet and the Italian-strung curtain is edged with crystal beaded trim.

This simple but elegant design is lovely in a bedroom in soft pastel silk.

A scrolled carved pelmet. The under-curtains close, the over-curtains are dress curtains.

An elaborate carved pelmet and deep valance, suitable for a stately home.

This complicated heading is teamed with a simple printed voile curtain.

Traditional

A single swag with tasselled ropes instead of tails.

Simple design in silk with a double swag and crystal trims, suitable for a bedroom.

A slotted heading like this is only suitable for dress curtains, as these curtains would not be able to open.

The studded, box-pleated heading gives this contemporary curtain design a traditional look.

Contrasting goblet pleats across the heading, each trimmed with a tassel to finish.

Elegant goblet headed curtains with dramatic jet beads on the base of the goblets and partially trimmed with jet fringing.

Here the main curtain is only a dress curtain, but the under-curtain does draw.

A different damask is used for each curtain, but both are lined with a bold striped silk.

Traditional

In formal settings there are often two windows side-by-side – here is one way to treat them.

Twin windows can also be dressed with a curtain each, but styled as a pair.

Draped pelmets always look dramatic, whether with one curtain...

... or teamed with two curtains.

Modern

A formal pelmet, but with a twist – made in a bold
spotted fabric and teamed with wide stripe curtains.

Modern

A versatile design because you can alter the look by changing the items hanging from the valance.

This valance has studded box pleats and a wide border top and bottom to accentuate its shape, which is echoed in the border at the hem of the curtain.

Plain and simple valance, but with a contrast rope trim to add interest.

A bias-cut valance falls in soft, attractive folds.

Stripes give a contemporary look to this design – and using a broad band of the fabric horizontally adds extra flair.

Create a tonal variation by using three different fabrics in bands – place the darkest tone at the bottom.

When using contrasting fabrics in squares, you can play about with the layout of colours to create your own geometric design.

On this giant stripe curtain the tabs are cut to the width of the stripe for a co-ordinated look.

Modern

A single voile curtain with a braid machined on to create your own design. This is a great way to add something extra to a large loft window.

When you are using a wire tracking to hang your curtains, you must only use a lightweight fabric such as a voile.

Here the blind is functional, but the fabric is just draped artistically over the pole.

A simple panel of fabric takes on a whole new style with the addition of deep fringing at the hem.

Modern

The leather thonging used to hang this curtain is echoed by adding diagonal lines of leather thong lacing across the fabric.

A simple grid of saddle stitching in a contrast colour on a plain curtain.

The fabric used to trim this curtain matches the floral roller blind behind and gives a homely country-style feel.

Different fabrics can be combined in one set of curtains – but make sure either the colour or the design co-ordinates to hold the look together.

When making up curtains from blocks of fabric, you can alter the size of the blocks for extra interest.

Joining bands of contrast fabric means you can have the stripes any width that you choose.

Adding a scalloped leading edge creates an interesting frame for the window.

A pointed turnover heading to match the functional curtains.

Modern

For an over-the-top design use big, bold fabrics combined with a co-ordinating stripe.

A handkerchief-point spotted contrast top is echoed in the matching band at the hem of this curtain.

Patchwork curtains are a great way to use up leftover pieces of fabric.

Wide tucks at the hem of this curtain add weight both visually and in reality, so the curtain hangs beautifully.

Delicate tie-headed curtains with deep frilling on the hem.

An unstructured linen curtain is given extra interest with a crocheted lace hem, which is repeated along the base of the blind.

Short, striped curtains are fun and practical for a kitchen window.

A fun design using spots and stripes in matching colours.

Bay windows

These curtains are hung from a covered lathe – the centre curtain pulls both ways.

A made-to-measure modern steel pole allows for extra versatility when dressing bay windows.

This French door in a deep recess has simple curtains on the outside of the recess, with a valance that runs right round the inside.

The curtain and valance on this bay recess are in a heavy dramatic fabric accentuated with deep bullion fringing.

Bay windows

Small bays need simple curtains – but the repeating bands of tucks at the base add some extra interest to this design.

Traditional and Modern Designs

When there are window seats, as in this case, just have dress curtains and functional blinds.

Blinds can be designed to co-ordinate exactly with the curtains – here they are made in the same fabric as the decorative band on the curtain and have the same bobble fringing.

If there is seating under the window, blinds on their own are often the best option.

Bay windows

Traditional
and Modern
Designs

Dramatic striped blinds are echoed in the contrast stripe on the dress curtain and valance.

Dress curtains with multi-coloured rope tie-backs and a co-ordinating deep fringe on the valance. The colours of the rope are picked up in the stripes of the blinds.

Another option for a bay window is to use two-tiered wooden shutters.

Roller blinds look more finished with a pelmet or valance – here they are teamed with a quilted pelmet.

Italian stringing

Use the biggest print you can find for this design.

The spotted lining is visible when the curtains are drawn back.

A goblet pleat heading on Italian-strung curtains – but these should stay fixed, only the blind is used.

A simple curtain design with an elaborate carved pelmet.

An Italian-strung under-curtain teamed with a softly draped dressed curtain.

Here the Italian-strung curtain is co-ordinated with the voile beneath by adding a wide band of curtain material as a border.

A cosy seating area is made more private with a simple Italian-strung curtain.

Italian-strung dress curtain with a scroll-printed roller blind.

Covered lathes

A covered lathe is essential for a window this unusual shape.

A covered lathe is very neat in a bay window.

One-sided curtain in black and white spotted silk, with a black covered lathe.

Here the striped contrast used on the leading edge matches the covered lathe.

Dressed curtains

If there are objects in the way of the window, such as
a window seat or raditator, you can still have dressed
curtains – just add a functional blind underneath.

Dressed curtains can be used in many ways – here are some more ideas for adding dressed curtains over functional blinds.

Voiles/sheers

Ribbon borders add a stylish touch to a plain voile panel.

A beautiful lace panel needs no more than a simple pole to display it.

A draped, one-sided top curtain with plenty of trimmings makes this voile design look stunning.

A one-sided top curtain adds a touch of formality to this simple voile.

Patterned voile teamed with a toning valance on a slotted heading.

For a less formal look, hang the voiles on hooks and loops.

This valance is made from an old shawl, knotted to the pole.

Points trimmed with tassels and gay stripes and checks are a fun look for a children's room.

Voiles/sheers

Traditional
and Modern
Designs

The wide braid used on the hem of these voiles is echoed in the lattice pattern on the pelmet.

Add bands of different lace trimmings and a simple fringe on the hem.

This voiles are tied with ribbons to the pole and matching ribbon is used to trim the hem.

Spotted Italian-strung voile curtains under a draped over-curtain.

A simple curtain design with added greenery for a garden room.

This plain curtain is made special by using a wide jacquard ribbon on the hem.

Gathered voile combined with a formal valance and co-ordinated with heavy fringing.

Plain voile panel with a heavy fringed shawl tied to the pole as a valance.

6

Alternatives to Curtains

Introduction to curtain alternatives...

There are alternatives...

Some people choose not to have curtains or blinds to cover their windows. There is no real reason for them — although it is rather nice to draw the curtains at night, rather like the end of a play, the day is over. It is cosier too and does help to make the room feel warmer. In the age of double glazing, perhaps it is just a habit, but some windows look unfinished without something to dress them up.

Some people can't sleep if there is a flicker of light in the room — in which case light resistant blinds behind the curtains are the answer. Kitchens and bathrooms look great with wooden shutters, and a wonderful old screen would give privacy but allow lots of light to stream in above. Here are a few window coverings that might look good in your home and are easy to make as well.

Panels

Panels are so versatile. They not only look good but also provide a cheaper alternative to curtaining as they use less fabric. The panels hang from tracking fixed on the ceiling and can be operated electronically. Although the cost of the ceiling tracking is high, eventually some manufacturer will come out with a cheaper version. Panels are used in many offices where the windows are large. It is best if there is enough 'stack back' either side of the window, so that when the panels are open they can be stored at the side to allow plenty of light into the room. There are several panel designs on the next few pages and you will see that there are various permutations: either with one big panel if the window is not too wide, or in sets of two or three.

Café and short curtains

Café curtains are generally are made with a slotted heading and hung on a rod about halfway up the window. They are used mainly to give a little privacy — they were invented to screen diners sitting in the window from people passing on the street, while still allowing them to look out. They are useful in a domestic situation for a similar reason, perhaps if the front of a house is right on the pavement so people can look in as they walk past. Old-fashioned cafés often use them in lace or gingham to create an old-world atmosphere. In America they seem to be particularly popular.

   In general, I am not a fan of short curtains, but sometimes they are the best option — on a door for instance, or for a cottage interior.

Dormer windows

The two problems with dormer windows is that they are often quite small and the top of the window or the ceiling above is a strange shape — either sloping or pointed. Since you will want to leave as much of the window clear as possible to let in light, and the top of any treatment has to be fixed, the options become somewhat limited. However, there are some things you can do that will look very acceptable — see pages 162–3 for some possible solutions to the problem.

Difficult windows

It is often best just to leave difficult windows alone if they are very odd shapes – it can look very silly to try to cover a strange shape with a piece of fabric and hope that it works. So unless the window has to have curtains for some important reason – privacy or to screen daylight – just leave it without any window dressing at all. However, if you must have something, there are a few ideas shown on pages 164–71 that may help to solve your problem window.

Window dressing

Dressing a window using unusual items can be great fun and there are hundreds of ways to do it. Some windows benefit from a little bit of dressing up – just putting some simple muslin up at the glass will defuse the light coming into the room. Other decorative ideas include stained glass, coloured marbles, pebbles and strips of coloured ribbon.

Remember, it is not necessary to cover every part of a window, especially if there is a spectacular view – why would you want to block out a great view with curtains?

Portières

Portières are generally one-sided curtains, which act as a door in a corridor – hence the name. They are pulled back to one side with a tie-back or hold-back, or may be Italian-strung. If the curtain needs to be closed on occasion, the first option is better.

The term portière can also be used to describe window or door coverings with a slotted heading top and bottom, in which the fabric is slotted onto rods attached at one side of the window only. The portière can then swing open and closed as required, for access to the window.

Panels

A sliding panel is an ideal solution to achieve some privacy.

For a wide window, three or more panels can stack and slide.

Braid and deep bullion fringe are repeated in the other soft furnishings nearby for a co-ordinated look.

Panels don't have to be plain – use large, important trims down the leading edge.

Panels

Simple trimmings add some extra style.

Ribbons and braids can be combined for a unique look.

A chevron border looks simple and modern.

The curves in the paisley print fabric band are echoed in the scalloped edge at the top of this panel.

Bold checks look best on a large picture window in a modern setting.

A single panel has a design of appliquéd squares and a matching border.

Panels

Panels that don't match create a sense of fun and frivolity.

Mondrian style for a set of French doors.

Large bold stripes are very effective on a single panel.

Huge chevrons need a modern bold interior, such as a loft apartment.

Eyelet holes and string lacing give a nautical look.

Lace inset bands create a softer, more romantic feeling.

Panels

A single panel shows off the design of this beautiful lace.

A translucent panel with scattered appliqué leaves gives privacy without losing too much light.

Covering the window panel with wallpaper to match the walls will create a streamlined feel for a simple interior.

Panels are great for a boy's room – a wipe-clean surface will allow them to express their creativity!

Using sliding panels across an alcove is a cheaper option than having a wardrobe made – and you can ring the changes by replacing the fabric with a different print.

Sliding panels are fun and practical to hide the clutter in a child's room.

Short/café curtains

Café curtains are ideal for a window next to a door to add a touch of privacy.

Slotted headings are best for café curtains that normally will not be drawn aside.

Hooks and loops are another option for a fixed café curtain.

Inverted pleats and braid trim create a stylish feel.

Knotting a scarf or fabric panel onto the pole is a neat option.

An unstructured heading and pulled back corner revealing a contrast lining gives a much softer look.

A gingham border and ties are ideal for a cottage interior.

A fabric panel on hooks over a glass door panel gives privacy.

For a more dressy option, use a miniature curtain complete with tabbed heading and tucked hem.

Dormer windows

Alternatives
to Curtains

Roman blind shaped into the point of the ceiling above the dormer.

A blind is the best option for a window covering in a confined space.

When adding a valance to a blind, make sure it sits high enough so it does not block out too much light.

The translucent panel in the centre of this London blind lets in extra light.

Here, the fabric panel trimmed with bobbles is just for fun, and the curtain is functional.

Matching windows look good with matching Oriental blinds.

Difficult windows

A fixed pleated pelmet over a
Roman blind.

Roman blinds are an ideal solution
with an unusually shaped window.

This Roman blind has a shaped top
which is held in place with studs.
The Roman blind is attached.

A long, thin window looks stylish
with a lambrequin teamed with a
shaped roller blind and pull tassel.

Sandblasted glass is a good solution
for a bathroom, offering privacy but
maximum natural light.

When fitting a blind into an unusual shape, make an accurate template in paper first.

The scalloped curves of this Austrian blind echo the curved centre of the window shape.

With roller blinds, anything is possible!

A stepped pelmet follows the shape of the stairs beneath.

Difficult windows

Swags and tails on a formal arched window.

An exotic stencil does away with the need for any other window dressing.

A shaped pelmet teamed with swags and tails for a really formal look.

Try teaming a lambrequin with lightweight Italian-strung curtains.

A decorative border and Italian-strung curtains with goblet heading.

Folding shutters are a good option if curtains are not suitable.

Double folding shutters on a small, wide window over a radiator.

Free-standing four-panel screen used instead of curtain or blinds.

A four-panel screen can be a temporary or a permanent solution.

Alternatives/other options

Alternatives
to Curtains

Display pebbles, shells or glass balls on the cross bars of a multi-paned window.

A linen portière opens out easily when necessary, but holds a panel of fabric taut over the window.

Stained glass is a long-term solution for a hard-to-get-at window.

Hanging panels on a tension rod – ring the changes by switching the panels around.

Lengths of beaded ribbon in differing designs and colours for a fun look.

A simple fabric panel folded up and held with ribbon ties is quick and easy to make.

For an instant solution, knot an old shawl to the pole.

Seasonal foliage brings a natural look into the interior.

A bagged-out swag and tail draped over the curtain pole.

Traditional portières

A lovely carved wooden pelmet is combined with an exciting mix of spots and flowers in this double portière curtain.

Use a big tassel fringe on this Italian-strung portière curtain.

For a true over-the-top-look, use as many strings of beads as possible.

A heavy, thick tweed portière with deep wool fringing – in case you live in a castle!

Modern portières

These sheer half-panels give some privacy, but still allow lots of light into the area.

A pretty, dotted sheer portière dresses the window, but is easy to open when necessary.

Portières are ideal for a bathroom, allowing the window to be opened for ventilation.

A simple linen portière with embossed initials for a personal touch.

An opening panel allows a wonderful view to be admired when privacy is not needed.

Translucent portières have a distinctly Japanese flavour.

Obscuring glass panels in the door can be difficult – a portière is one possible solution.

Dressing a window

This pretty sheer fabric has a lovely trim weighted with drop crystals.

A fretwork pelmet gives a simple and stylish look all on its own.

This half blind edged with chevrons is ideal for the kitchen.

174

Dress blind with a chevron-pointed hem trimmed with lace and tassels.

Sometimes curtains are not required at all for a great look.

Wonderful strings of crystals, hung in a carefully graded diagonal.

A pretty valance trimmed with a wide band of lace is all this window needs.

175

7

Blinds

Introduction to blinds...

A few words of advice...
There are a few instances where blinds don't work –
if the windows are not suitable for blinds for some
reason then more than likely they will not be right for
curtains either. So I would generally just dress the
window so that it doesn't look bare, and move on!

Roman blinds

This type of blind is a softer version of the roller blind;; it hangs
flat when it is in the down position and folds neatly up into
horizontal pleats when it is in the up position. The blind is fixed
to a covered batten with the aid of 'touch and close' tape
(known in the UK as Velcro®) and operated by lift cords which
pass through the china barrels secured by brass, chrome or
wooden cleats. You can have a right or left side operation.

   Roman blinds tend to be the most popular type of blind,
mainly because they are uncluttered and therefore suit most
room schemes. They are often lined and even interlined
depending upon the type of fabric being used. Use them
unlined in place of the old-fashioned 'net' curtains used for
privacy.

Austrian blinds

If like me you don't particularly like these blinds you will still find
some clients insisting on them. They are very fussy but do fit
into a formal setting very well. I use them sometimes with a
simple dressed curtain or a panel and that looks quite good. You
will find a few examples throughout the book.

Linen fold

These blinds are completely unstructured and I like the way
they fit so well into a contemporary setting. There are no poles
or rods and, unlike Roman blinds, they are not 'trained' and
therefore fall in a relaxed style. As the centre fabric is often
voile or an open weave, avoid having any seams across the
fabric or this can look a mess. So the maximum width of your
blind will be the width of your fabric, which is generally about
180cm (72in) but there is no restriction on length. The borders
have to be a more solid fabric, such as linen, as there are eyelet
holes down the side for the cords to run through, which when
pulled makes the blind go up into folds.

Cascades

These are quite formal and are similar to Romans but when
they are in the down position they stay in their folds. A Cascade
is handmade and attached to a covered batten and, like the
Roman blind, it is operated by the same cording system. The
pleats retain their shape by the steel rods inserted into the
horizontal pockets at the back of the blind. Avoid using cascades
in bay windows, as they tend to be a bit bulky.

Oriental blinds

Very basic blinds and easy to make. They simply roll up and down by cords which pass through rings; the cords can be in contrast colours or matched to the top fabric. Normally the Oriental blind is 'bagged' out – this means that there are two fabrics, one for the front and one for the contrast at the back, machined together on the wrong side and then turned inside out – therefore, the quantities of fabric are equal. It is a good idea to add a machine hem stitch to the edge of the two fabrics because if the fabric is too thick the blind will not roll up and down smoothly. If you are having them unlined you must have French seams, as the seams will show when rolled and will look unsightly from the outside when in the down position.

London blinds

These are quite formal blinds and are best used in a formal setting. The blinds should be lined and interlined (not too heavy) with a contrast colour fabric for the inverted pleats. Used mainly to dress a window, for instance in a hall or on a landing, but be careful as this blind has to be well made and positioned properly or it can look disastrous. They are very useful for arched windows, as the top of the blind can be shaped to fit almost any shape of window – but you will obviously need to give the manufacturer a template to follow.

Shutters

These are my favourite type of blinds. They are the most versatile of all window coverings. They are not cheap, but I think they are worth every penny you spend on them. Make sure you go to a good manufacturer, as there are many cheap copies and they will always cause problems. They are permanently fixed to the windows and can be hinged back completely or left in situ and the louvres moved to the open or closed position manually. By moving the louvres to the open position you can fine tune the amount of light you want in the room. Shutters can be spray painted any colour or you can have them made in various types of wood such as mahogany, beech, pine, cherry or oak. The louvres come in several sizes the most popular are 4.8cm ($1\frac{7}{8}$in), 6.4cm ($2\frac{1}{2}$in) or 8.9cm ($3\frac{1}{2}$in) but each manufacturer has their own specific sizes. Always make sure that the middle rails match your window frame. Shutters work really well in bay windows and can be custom made to any shape of window. They are especially good in conservatories, for Velux® windows and can also be used as wardrobe doors. I buy my shutters for my clients from a particular manufacturer who plants a tree for every order for shutters – nice thought!

Blinds

Basic blinds

Roller blind

Roman blind

Austrian blind

Oriental blind

Linen fold blind

Cascade blind

London blind

Roman blind for slanting window

Basic roller blinds

These were the first blinds on the market and during the last few years have gone out of fashion, but they seem to be coming back in a big way now. They are very versatile, suitable for most windows, and can be dressed up in many ways to suit different situations.

If you use a translucent fabric, these roller blinds can replace those old-fashioned-looking 'net' curtains, letting in natural light but still giving a certain amount of privacy.

If you are thinking of having light-resistant lining in your bedroom curtains to stop the light coming in, then use light-resistant roller blinds in the windows instead and cover them with a flimsy curtain to soften the look – it works much better.

Roller blinds can be rolled either way – these are 'reverse rolled', meaning that the blind is not close to the window. This is useful in kitchens where condensation could spoil the blind.

Cleat   Correct way to wind the cord when blind is in the 'up' position.

Selection of cord pulls.

Curtains with blinds

A pretty sheer curtain dresses the window, but the scalloped blind behind cuts out light and provides full privacy.

Blind trimmed with crystal fringing to match the curtain.

Lovely unstructured curtain pulled to one side and tied with a big satin bow, over a crenellated blind with a pull bar.

Blinds

Roller blinds

Combining fabrics offers many variations, such as this chequerboard...

... or this inset square.

Roller blinds don't have to have a pull cord – this one has a metal pull bar.

A simple roller blind can look stunning in the right fabric.

Try combining the blind with a lambrequin.

A fretwork pelmet looks very stylish.

Roller blinds are ideal in the kitchen – try using a co-ordinating border.

Using insets and braids means you can create your own unique design.

A translucent roller blind will let in some light.

Lambrequins

Simple curved lambrequin in striped fabric.

Shaping the arch adds an extra decorative element to this scroll fabric lambrequin.

Any shape can be made... this one adds a curve that contrasts with the plaid fabric.

Diagonal stripes on this pointed arch lambrequin.

Fretwork lambrequins

Points and curves work well together.

Carved and scrollwork lambrequin in wood.

Roman blinds

Simple stripes for a minimalist interior.

Lush brocade fabric for the period look.

Stripes and a bold border work in this country interior.

Japanese cherry blossom adds an Oriental look to this kitchen.

Roman blinds

Bold brickwork-design in Russian braid gives a sharp modern look.

Matching chequerboard blinds look smart on a double window.

A bold geometric print makes this Roman blind a major feature of the room.

Pretty lace Roman blinds are ideal to soften this modern bathroom.

With valances

Roman blind with plain tabbed valance.

Multi-fabric Roman blind with tied valance for a pretty, informal look.

Scalloped valance trimmed with a matching border.

Soft tucked valance on rings, trimmed with a lace border.

Tucked valance over saddle-stitched Roman blind.

Shaped valance to fit into a pointed window.

With valances

The layered look – bands of different fabric on the blind topped with another for the valance.

This blind is edged with a wide jacquard ribbon, as is the matching valance.

Masculine plaids are softened with this gathered valance.

Austrian blinds

Giant polka dots and gingham trim look great on gathered fabric.

Sheer Austrian blind with fretwork pelmet.

The pretty rose print on this blind matches the carved roses on the pelmet.

Bold stripes and a Greek key pelmet for the Empire look.

Matching fabric for blinds, stool and tablecloth for a co-ordinated look.

Simple gingham with a bobble fringe is great for a nursery.

A richly patterned fabric gives a lush feel to this shaped blind.

Sheer lace makes a great blind that will let light into the room even when down.

Austrian blinds

A beautiful silk blind with heavy crystal trimming.

A slotted heading on a voile blind with contrast frilling.

Traditional-looking design with plenty of ropes and tassels.

Translucent fabric lets in light, but the pencil pleat heading adds a touch of formality.

With curtains or panels

A dress curtain and co-ordinating blind.

Bright plaids for blind and curtain give a cheerful Scottish look.

Sliding panels in a range of fabrics – the curves of the matching blind soften the geometric effect.

Giant prints look good on panels, but would be lost on the gathered fabric of a blind.

Linen folds

Canvas, eyelets and rope for a touch of the seaside...

... and teamed with gingham for a country feel.

A valance with a slotted heading and bobble fringe teamed with a simple linen fold blind.

Linen folds are great for a country interior.

Checked border to match the tiled frieze in this kitchen.

In this modern, minimalist bathroom a curtain would be too fussy.

Lights on either side of this window leave no room for a curtain.

Windows on stairs always look better with a blind rather than a curtain.

Cascades

Using different fabrics adds variety and interest and creates an informal look. Here, the top panel matches the wall frieze.

Stripes of bold colour co-ordinate with the wall frieze – make sure the width of the top panel lines up with the edges of the frieze.

Blinds

This shaped lambrequin gives an Eastern feel to the design.

Using a simple curved lambrequin and Russian braid gives a more military look.

A shawl draped over the pole softens the angular feel of a blind.

Draped fabric creates an informal swag and tails.

A fretwork pelmet conceals and finishes off the top of a cascade blind.

Here, the ironwork pelmet has a matching design at the sill.

Cascades

Cascade blinds look good in a recessed window.

Add a slotted valance trimmed with tassel fringing for a more luxurious look.

A formal setting demands a more formal treatment – such as this complex double valance trimmed with rope.

A heavy fabric pelmet and valance, trimmed with matching rope and bullion fringe, add gravitas to this design.

Stunning fabric combined with a triangular point hem embellished with tassels.

A stencilled pelmet is a great option for a child's room. Two smaller matching blinds are a better option in this situation than one large one.

Create a calm, Oriental feel with this shaped pelmet combined with cascade blind and panels.

Panels combined with blinds are a less fussy option than curtains.

Oriental blinds

Oriental blinds are the easiest blinds to make. Line the panel with a contrast fabric for a great effect.

Florals combined with gingham are a soft and pretty option.

A dramatic chevron design is backed with a plain, strong colour.

An Oriental blind is ideal to control the light in a work area.

Translucent Oriental blinds provide privacy without cutting down on natural light.

Matching windows with matching plain Oriental blinds are very effective.

A fretwork pelmet and a contrast-lined over-curtain make this simple blind look more dressy.

Japanese sliding paper panels and cherry blossom printed on the blind for a truly Oriental look.

London blinds

The boldly printed floral fabric is displayed to advantage on this London blind, which is teamed with a pencil-pleated valance.

A strongly contrasting border accentuates the shape of this blind and its valance.

Blinds are an ideal option for arched windows...

... of all types. Here, the braided trim highlights the curve of the window shape.

A traditional London blind with rope trim to the pelmet and matching tasselled fringe.

An unusual chevron pelmet echoes the chevron design of the dado frieze.

A plain design, but the strips of ribbon and bows on the pelmet add a charming touch.

The inverted pleats on valance and blind are lined with a contrasting fabric.

Shutters

Shutters are a great option for French doors – make sure they open the opposite way to the doors.

Whatever the window shape, a shutter can be made to fit.

Two-tier shutters allow the option of having one or the other level open for more light while still giving a certain amount of privacy.

Half shutters offer privacy but maximum natural light.

Angular shapes are quite possible with shutters.

With sloping ceilings, the shutter can be fixed but with moveable slats to control the light.

Extra-wide slats look stylish in a modern bathroom.

A fixed shutter panel in the arch, with opening shutters for the window beneath – a very classical look.

Wooden and metal Venetians

Simple wooden Venetian blinds look stunning in black.

Triple window with three matching wooden Venetian blinds.

Metal Venetian blinds look simple and stylish in a modern interior.

Venetian blinds are ideal for those odd situations where other treatments won't work.

The webbing on Venetian blinds can be a matching or a contrasting colour.

Try painting the slats to match the colours in the interior.

Velux® blinds

Rooflights such as Velux® windows need blinds specially made with the correct fixings.

Another Velux® blind – ideal in bathrooms.

8

Beds

Introduction to beds...

A few words of advice...
Your bed is the most important piece of furniture in your home. Don't try to economize in any way. Buy your bed from a good department store with a proper bed department where the staff are trained to advise you. Buy a good make like Hypnos, Staples, Vi-Spring or Reylon. These manufacturers know about beds, as they have been in the business for a long time.

Bedcovers

These are not as popular as they used to be, as most people now prefer to have a duvet. There are such pretty duvet covers that there is no need to have a bedcover as well. On page 216, I have just shown one shape and some variations for if you prefer a bedcover. On page 217, I have given you some ideas for designs with valances.

Headboards

Fabric headboards can be made in many, many different shapes. Every now and again the fashion changes and so do the headboards! Most of my clients at the moment like to have very tall ones; I am not sure why this is but, as I say, it's the fashion.

Iron headboards look nice although they can be uncomfortable – but I suppose you have to have a little discomfort if you want to get the right look!

Wooden headboards can be homemade to give a rustic feel to the bedroom or they can be sophisticated carved Louis XIV copies. Modern wooden beds often have the headboard incorporated into the frame and the mattress is laid on top of wooden slats – very uncomfortable!

Coronas

These are like a coronet over the bed and generally have a valance edged with some kind of trimming. Then a pair of dress curtains come from under the corona and they are draped over a hold-back or hook either side of the headboard.

Canopies

A canopy is a piece of fabric draped over a bed purely for effect. If you are fixing it to the ceiling, be sure you find a secure fixing to take the weight.

Half tester and four-poster

A half tester is like a corona, but it goes the whole width of the bed. Curtains are fixed from the half tester and they fall neatly behind the headboard.

Four-poster beds nearly always have curtains around them. This originated from the need to keep warm or for privacy. With a traditional four-poster there is often a very elaborate silk dressing above the bed with pin tucks and pleats. This is a good opportunity to use trimmings on the edge of the valance and the curtains are held back to the four posts with tassel tie-backs. Modern four-posters are made in wood, steel or in fact anything goes. The curtains are not so formal and are sometimes casually just thrown over the frame.

Children's bedrooms

Bedrooms for children need to have plenty of storage boxes and book shelves. A nice idea is to incorporate a workstation into the room somehow. Little girls' rooms need more hanging space and boys need shelving for their football gear. It is fun to give the room a theme that can be changed as the child grows up.

Buying a bed

Dos

1 Lie on the bed in the shop, properly, with your eyes shut, and really think about the comfort. Nobody will laugh at you, and if they do so what! You are going to sleep on this bed half your life so get it right.

2 Buy a summer duvet with 4.5 tog upwards and a winter one with 10.5 tog upwards. Remember to have your duvets cleaned regularly and hang them on the clothes line to air once a month.

3 Choose your pillows carefully. I never bothered with anything special, a pillow is a pillow I thought, but a friend told me about her goose down pillow and how well she slept and I thought I would go into my local store and buy one for myself as an experiment. Well, I have never looked back. I can't believe that most of my long life I have been sleeping on rubbish pillows when all the time there was a goose down pillow waiting to whisk me off to dreamland!

4 Buy a topper to go on top of your mattress, however good your mattress is you still should go for a topper. You can get them now in the UK but originally I think they were only available in US. A topper is simply a mattress cover; it is generally quilted and stuffed with down. It feels as if you are lying on a feather bed, which is divine but real feather beds are not very good for your back.

5 Have a cashmere or knitted blanket at the bottom of the bed for those chilly nights – it's lovely to cuddle up to in the middle of the night!

6 Have a padded headboard for comfort – wooden and iron ones look great, but they are not for sitting in bed reading the Sunday papers!

7 Spend just a little extra and buy Egyptian cotton sheets or duvet covers. I know they need ironing but the difference in feel is worth it.

Don'ts

1 Don't buy a bed with storage under the mattress, as then the base is hard with no springs, so no matter how much you spend on a mattress the bed is always going to be hard.

2 Don't pay extra for an orthopaedic bed just because you think it is the smart thing to do. If you have a bad back you may need one for medical reasons, but generally people just feel it guarantees a good bed. But why pay double the price for an orthopaedic label when most manufacturers have a type of orthopaedic mattress in their range at half the price?

3 Valances to match 'non iron' sheets. Have one made just to cover the bed base in the same fabric as your curtains or bedspread – it looks much better and is worth the extra money.

4 Don't have your bed with its back to the light. Try to arrange the room so you can look out of the window as it can be quite depressing with the light behind you and if you are lucky enough to have a view you won't be able to see it!

5 Black satin sheets – that look is over and have you ever tried to iron them?

6 Avoid very heavy blankets on the bed; it is better to have a duvet or sheets with soft knitted blankets. Heavy blankets can make you feel quite claustrophobic in the night.

Beds

Headboards

Basic shape

Cut-out shape

Raised centre

Half moon

Pointed

Wood and fabric

Modern

Alternative

Beds

214

Bedcovers

A basic throwover bedspread.

Bedcovers are ideal for bold prints, as the large area means they are displayed to advantage.

A quilted cover decorated with American knots.

Knotted ties made from the same fabric as the border.

Valances

Inverted pleats with ties – carry the tied theme onto the pillow too.

Valance with inverted pleats.

Pretty gathered and scalloped edge valance.

Simple striped box valance.

Padded headboards

A tall padded headboard.

Studded headboard with lights and base to match.

Beds

A low, thick headboard with a screen behind to complete the look.

A fun bed using lots of colourful fabrics.

These headboards look like two giant cushions – and they are very comfortable.

A padded headboard in a very traditional shape.

A ruched, traditional-shaped headboard.

Wooden

Traditional carved bedframes come in a variety of styles.

Country-style wooden bedframes.

Contemporary

Modern wooden bedframe with two headboards.

Slotted wooden headboard with a curved top.

Ebony bedframe with curved headboard and square feet for an Oriental look.

Contemporary bedframe with wooden surround.

Iron

Traditional Victorian iron bedstead with brass finials.

Modern version of the Victorian metal bedstead.

Iron bedstead with brass detailing.

Wrought iron bedstead with pretty leaf details.

Iron

High posts at the bedhead to hold a curtain.

Cast floral detailing in typical antique French style.

A modern four-poster looks just as good without any curtaining.

Or you can add curtains for a softer look.

Coronas

The crystal fringing on the corona and bed curtain is repeated on the bed throw.

This corona has a triple pleat heading with square buttons and deep fringing.

The fabric used for this pinch-pleated corona is also used to line the bed curtain.

A light and pretty corona of wrought metal, with French-style voile curtains.

The classic corona looks best in a period property.

A formal daybed with heavily fringed corona and softly draped curtain.

Half testers

Bold floral curtains and ribbon borders give this half tester a more contemporary look.

The triangle point-edged pelmet with tassels evokes a medieval feel.

Traditional half tester with carved pelmet, heavy curtains and tasselled tie-backs.

A simplified traditional look, with draped curtains. The deep fringing on the valance is repeated on the bedcover.

Ostrich feathers and a heavily carved and tented pelmet give an opulent look to this half tester.

A pair of half tester beds in simple fabrics – a modern treatment that would not look out of place in a very traditional interior.

Traditional four-posters

Traditional four-posters are so over-the-top anyway that you can get away with using lots of wonderful trimmings.

Heavy crystal fringing accentuates the curving shape of the valance. The rope of the tie-backs is also used to trim the curtains, headboard, bolster and bedcover.

Four-poster with full curtains only at the bedhead for a less overpowering effect.

Some wooden four-posters have such beautifully turned pillars that it would be a crime to hide them with curtaining.

The outline shape of the pelmet to this four-poster echoes the carving on the headboard.

Softly draped unstructured curtains and a tented ceiling contrast with the bold masculine posts of this ebony four-poster.

Pretty fabric twisted loosely around the posts and allowed to pool on the floor for a softer, more feminine look.

Modern four-posters

A simple ebony four-poster.

A metal frame creates a stunning look.

A modern version of a traditional four-poster, with muslin drapes.

This bamboo four-poster echoes Far Eastern designs.

A Japanese-inspired metal frame.

Canopy

A draped canopy.

An imaginative way to use mosquito netting.

Traditional mosquito netting.

A double headboard with simple canopy.

The end of the canopy can be rolled down.

A really original canopy, made from chains and draped fabric.

Children's

A canopy over a child's cot creates a small, private world.

Wooden cots can be carved into all sorts of shapes – such as this teddy bear cot.

Ribbons, lace and a throw with a knotted fringe for this charming four-poster.

Boldly striped bedcover and football motifs make this the quintessential boy's room.

Beds

Children's

The blinds create a great hideaway when down, but can be pulled up and out of the way. The bed itself contains plenty of storage for childhood treasures.

Child-size wooden four-poster.

An alcove bed is ideal for a child's room and can be dressed as a seating unit during the daytime.

A bunk bed over a study area is a compact and practical use of space.

Children's bedrooms

Three-tiered curtains using a different fabric for each tier.

A slotted heading with lace inserts.

A single panel with a band of wallpaper to match the motif on the wall.

A box-pleated heading with studs and checked lining to match the wallpaper.

Children's bedrooms

A pretty window treatment with a roller blind behind it.

This linen fold is placed over the recessed window.

An iron shepherd's pole with tiny pinch-pleated heading.

A casual heading on the curtain and a pointed soft pelmet decorated with bells.

Accessories

9

Introduction to accessories...

Accessorizing with style...
Sometimes it is the accessories that just make the scheme. If you have a fairly bland background palette, colourful accessories can make all the difference. And you can change them easily at little expense.

Table covers

These are easy to make and can be layered with several cloths or even just be a simple round piece of fabric perhaps with some kind of trimming on the edge. They can be lined and even interlined to allow them to fall well – but this is for formal room settings, the trend now is for a more casual look. The following pages will give you some ideas.

Screens

Screens are very useful to divide a room, create a cosy corner, protect you from a draught or just to add a touch of extra decoration to a room. They are the latest accessory and are very handy in a whole host of situations. Hand painted or upholstered, in leather or in silk, there is no end to the combinations and their versatility.

Cushions

Cushions continue to be popular and you can never have too many of them. They do tend to be larger now and scatter cushions are a thing of the past.

I tend to try to find a theme for the cushions so that they tie in with the decor but don't look too contrived. For instance, if they are on a big settee with blankets thrown over them for a casual look I would have some knitted ones and perhaps a couple of suede ones all in muted colours – I hate bright cushions!

Throws

Throws were originally meant to be rugs to throw over you if you were feeling a bit chilly, but now they are everywhere and come in all shapes and sizes. You can buy inexpensive ones, or those costing a fortune. I have a simple cashmere rug in London and a Welsh blanket in the country – nothing too pretentious for me!

Rugs

Rugs are my most favourite accessory. I prefer to have wide plank wooden floors everywhere in a flat or a house. In this way you can cover the floors with wonderful pure wool rugs and change the rugs every so often if you get bored with them.

Most stores have a huge supply of rugs from countries around the world – there is something to suit every taste. If you are working on a large project, such as a hotel, you can always have bespoke ones made – and there are companies who can make one-off designs for smaller projects, but at a price, of course.

Flowers

Flowers can change the feel of a room. They bring colour into the room if that is what is needed or they can 'pretty' a room up if that is what is missing.

Personally I do dislike silk flowers, but they are sometimes quite amazing. If they are used sparingly and mixed in with something natural – say autumn leaves, for instance – the effect does look very respectable.

Table covers

A collection of table covers, which can be made in mixed fabrics or perhaps in the same fabric as any curtains or cushions in the room.

Mix prints and add beads to give some added interest — but remember that if you include any trimmings, the table covers must be dry cleaned.

Screens

Screens are useful for many reasons – I use them sometimes instead of curtains, to keep out a draught or to make a picture.

Cushions and throws

Using trims is a great way to add a
unique style to plain cushions.

Black and white always wins...

Cotton checks, polka dots and floral prints are the essence of country style.

Throws and Welsh blankets are ideal to cover up boring fabrics and add instant chic.

Cushions

Black Russian braid is ideal to create your own designs. Experiment with frogging, lacing, appliqué and bows.

Animal prints add an exotic touch.

You can't really beat a classic Missoni print; it's a very distinguished style that will be a classic for many generations to come.

Rustic tweeds are ideal for the country house look, and combine well with bullion fringe, giant buttons and leather straps.

Flowers

Flowers add instant dressing to any scheme. Match the selection to the interior style – here bold flowers are teamed with a wide stripe wallpaper.

Create interest in a dull corner by adding delicate blossom in a glass vase.

Three small arrangements in a row can look better than one larger arrangement.

Rugs

A dramatic rug design like this looks best in a plain interior with no clutter to detract from its impact.

There is a wide range of styles available on the market – from simple stripes to traditional floral, and all combinations in between.

Borders add a finishing touch to a rug and can be plain or patterned.

Skills and Techniques

Measuring

Make sure you use a metal retractable measure to avoid making mistakes at this point when accurate measuring is vital. Decisions have to be made before you measure, such as whether you are having a pole, tracking concealed by a covered lathe, a pelmet or a simple blind.

To measure accurately you should have the pole or whichever type of curtain tracking in position, in order to measure the drop (length) of the curtain correctly. Generally these are fixed about 20cm (8in) above the architrave, but this does vary greatly depending on the position of the window to the ceiling. Wooden poles should be 6.3cm (2½in) in diameter if the curtains are long and can be as thin as 2.5cm (1in) for voile curtains (sheers) or short ones.

Be sure to check the following...

- ► You have sketched a flat drawing of your window so that you can put the measurements on the outline for accuracy.
- ► Make sure you have chosen the right design for the window.
- ► Choose a suitable pole or tracking.
- ► Are you having a pelmet or valance? Check this is right for the window – will you block out too much light?
- ► Decide on the type of heading for your curtains.
- ► Check which way your windows open – if they open into the room be sure your chosen window coverings will clear the window when it is open.
- ► It is best to have a place to stack the curtains on either side of the window when the curtains are open, so you do not lose too much light during the day. Your pole should be fixed the whole width including the 'stack backs'.

- ► If you have to hang the curtains from the ceiling, be sure to find a fixing in a beam that will be strong enough to take the weight of the curtains.
- ► Start to measure up, using a retractable metal measure.
- ► The curtain pole, tracking or pelmet board should be in place before you take any measurements.
- ► As a general rule tracks or poles should be fixed about 20cm (8in) above the architrave, but this does vary greatly depending on the relationship of the window to the ceiling – this is where common sense comes into it!
- ► If you are using a pole for your curtains be sure to use the right thickness. If the curtains are long the pole should be at least 6.3cm (2½in) in diameter. For voile curtains or short curtains the pole can be thinner – maybe 2.5cm (1in) – but I would rather have the pole a bit too thick than too mean looking.

To achieve good results in your curtain-making projects you will need a few pieces of equipment, but most of the items are not expensive and you probably already have most of them in your sewing kit. Start by purchasing the essentials: needles, pins, tape measure, your choice of marking tools, dressmaker's shears, seam ripper. Buy the best you can afford and add other items as you need them.

You will need a sewing machine – although it is feasible to hand sew curtains, it is very hard work and will take a really long time, so why bother? If you don't have a sewing machine, try to borrow one. You only need a basic model – computerized functions and embroidery stitches are not necessary.

Essential equipment

Sewing machine – the most expensive piece of sewing equipment you will need to purchase is a sewing machine, so if you plan to buy one it is worth taking time to be sure you end up with one you like to use. If you don't have one already try to borrow one to make your first curtains – this will give you some idea of which functions you will actually need and which ones you will not. There is no point in paying for complex features that you may not understand and will probably never use. Try out different machines in the showroom and take full advantage of any professional instruction that may be offered. The instruction book will explain your specific machine, but most have some common features.

Dressmaker's scissors – these have blades at an angle to the handles, so the blade can slide along the worksurface when cutting and not lift the fabric much, which allows for more accurate cutting.

Pinking shears – these shears have notched blades so they cut a zigzag line, which is useful to trim raw seam edges to prevent fraying.

Embroidery scissors – the short, sharp blades of embroidery scissors are designed to trim threads. Do not use your fabric shears for this, as it will eventually blunt the blade.

Tape measure (flexible and metal retractable) – a flexible tape measure is useful to take measurements of fabric. Use a plastic or fibreglass one – the cloth ones are prone to stretch over time. The metal retractable tape is the ideal tool to take measurements of windows, as you can extend the measure way above your head.

Tailor's chalk – solid chalk for marking fabric often comes in a triangular shape for ease of use and can be used to make a range of line thicknesses.

Pins with coloured heads – the large coloured heads of these pins make them easy to spot when you need to remove them. Buy those with glass heads rather than plastic, which may melt if caught with an iron.

Sewing needles (all sizes) – ordinary sewing needles are commonly called sharps. Keep a selection in a range of sizes. Change your sewing machine needle regularly – a blunt needle will cause stitching problems.

Thimble – many people do not like to use a thimble, but if you do a lot of sewing you will soon get used to using it and it will save your fingers from damage.

Seam ripper – this special tool is invaluable – it has a sharp prong to push into stitches and a short curved blade to cut through them.

Thread – thread comes in a range of fibres, both natural and synthetic, and in many colours. It also comes in different thicknesses – the thicker threads are normally used for things like topstitching, where the stitches are designed to be seen as a feature.

Hem weights – these cone-like weights are sometimes known as penny or hem weights. They are used at the bottom corners and at the bottom of each joined seam. A small size is suitable for lightweight curtains, the larger heavier size is better for heavy fabric and full length curtains.

Touch and close tape (Velcro®) – this consists of two layers: a 'hook' side, which is a piece of fabric covered with tiny hooks, and a 'loop' side, which is covered with even smaller loops. When the two sides are pressed together, the hooks catch in the loops and hold the pieces together.

Eyelet hole kit – this consists of a punch to make the hole, and a setting tool to place and lock the two halves of the eyelet rings to seal the edges of the hole.

Tracing paper (I use parchment cooking paper) – useful to trace designs or transfer markings.

Steam iron – you will need to press seams open during the making process, and press hems. You can use your regular ironing surface and steam iron for this.

Weights – These are used to hold down lightweight fabrics while you cut them out.

Skills and Techniques

Measuring curtains

Measuring cut length curtains

For short curtains, measure from the ring on pole or track to 13cm (5in) below the sill ①. For long curtains, measure from the ring on pole or track to the floor ②, but add extra if you want the curtains to break on the floor.

Pelmets or valances – fix the pelmet board at the same height as you would a pole. The depth of the pelmet or valance should, as a rough guide, be one-sixth of the total height of the curtains, so divide the curtain height by six to find the correct depth ③. Add 13cm (5in) to allow for your heading and hem.

Measuring curtain width

Measure between the architraves ④ and add on an extra 30cm (12in) on each side to allow for stack-backs ⑤. Remember to add seam allowances.

Measuring up for blinds

Fix blinds approximately 20cm (8in) above the architrave to allow as much light as possible into the room. Measure the width between the architraves and add 5cm (2in) each side ⑥. To work out the length, measure the length of the window and add 20cm (8in) above the architrave plus 2.5cm (1in) below the sill ⑦.

Measuring up for curtains and blinds in recess

Measure the length from the top to the bottom of the recess. Measure the width of the recess. If you choose blinds, always remember to check the measurements at the top, middle and bottom as windows can be irregular. If the window is very small, it is preferable to hang curtains outside the recess to avoid losing too much light, or use a swing arm to hang the curtains.

Measuring up for swags and tails

For the swag length, measure the width of the pelmet board that is going to carry your tracking and add approximately 40cm (16in). To calculate the swag depth, multiply the required length by two. The inner edge of the tail should be the same length as the swag. The outer edge should be about three-quarters of the total curtain length.

Calculating fabric requirements

Divide the curtain width by the width of your fabric to find the number of curtain drops (lengths) required. Decide on the fullness you require. Traditional curtains should have 2–3 widths of fabric, unless the fabric is very thick, and the more contemporary styles are generally about two widths of fullness – see the section on fabric quantities on pages 266–8. Obviously curtain panels have no fullness at all. Multiply the number of drops by the cut length measurement to find the required amount of fabric – see the table on page 266. If your fabric has a pattern, allow one EXTRA pattern repeat for each drop.

Measuring blinds

Face fix

Recessed window

A The drop (length) from the top of the architrave to the sill.

B The drop (length) from 20cm (8in) above the architrave to just below the sill.

C The width if the blind is to be fixed on the architrave.

D The width if the blind is to overlap on either side.

E The top point is where a pole, pelmet or valance should be fixed – approx. 20cm (8in). The bottom point is the drop of the pelmet or valance.

A The drop (length).

B The width – take the measurement at the top, middle and near the bottom as windows can vary in a recess.

Fabric quantities for curtains/drapes

2½ x heading fullness
30cm heading and hem allowance, 2 x 7cm overlaps and 2 x 8cm returns

Measurements in metres

Length of track or pole up to									
120cm fabric	0.55	1.00	1.50	1.95	2.45	2.90	3.35	3.85	4.30
137cm fabric	0.70	1.20	1.75	2.30	2.85	3.35	3.90	4.45	5.00
150cm fabric	0.80	1.40	2.00	2.55	3.15	3.75	4.35	4.90	5.50

No. of widths	2	3	4	5	6	7	8	9	10
Finished Length									
1.80	4.20	6.30	8.40	10.50	12.60	14.70	16.80	18.90	21.00
1.90	4.40	6.60	8.80	11.00	13.20	15.40	17.60	19.80	22.00
2.00	4.60	6.90	9.20	11.50	13.80	16.10	18.40	20.70	23.00
2.10	4.80	7.20	9.60	12.00	14.40	16.80	19.20	21.60	24.00
2.20	5.00	7.50	10.00	12.50	15.00	17.50	20.00	22.50	25.00
2.30	5.20	7.80	10.40	13.00	15.60	18.20	20.80	23.40	26.00
2.40	5.40	8.10	10.80	13.50	16.20	18.90	21.60	24.30	27.00
2.50	5.60	8.40	11.20	14.00	16.80	19.60	22.40	25.20	28.00
2.60	5.80	8.70	11.60	14.50	17.40	20.30	23.20	26.10	29.00
2.70	6.00	9.00	12.00	15.00	18.00	21.00	24.00	27.00	30.00
2.80	6.20	9.30	12.40	15.50	18.60	21.70	24.80	27.90	31.00
2.90	6.40	9.60	12.80	16.00	19.20	22.40	25.60	28.80	32.00
3.00	6.60	9.90	13.20	16.50	19.80	23.10	26.40	29.70	33.00
3.10	6.80	10.20	13.60	17.00	20.40	23.40	27.20	30.60	34.00
3.20	7.00	10.50	14.00	17.50	21.00	24.50	28.00	31.50	35.00
3.30	7.20	10.80	14.40	18.00	21.60	25.20	28.80	32.40	36.00
3.40	7.40	11.10	14.80	18.50	22.20	25.90	29.60	33.30	37.00
3.50	7.60	11.40	15.20	19.00	22.80	26.60	30.40	34.20	38.00

To use this chart:

1 Find your fabric width at top right in the first column. Go along the line to the right of the fabric width to find the nearest measurement to the width of your track or pole – if this falls between two measurements, use the larger one.

2 Find the number of fabric widths you need by looking directly below your track or pole measurement in the No. of widths line.

3 The column below the number of widths shows the amount of fabric required to achieve a finished length of curtains as shown in the column on the far left.

Fabric quantities for valances

2½ x heading fullness
Valances can have more fullness in them than the accompanying curtains.
This fullness is suitable for most decorative headings, especially hand
box-pleated valances (although some machine tapes require 3 x fullness)
and smocked-headed valances.

15cm for heading and hem allowance
2 x 15cm returns for either pelmet board or valance rail

Measurements in metres

Length of pelmet board or valance rail up to

120cm fabric	0.60	1.05	1.50	2.00	2.45	2.95	3.40	3.90	4.35
137cm fabric	0.70	1.25	1.80	2.35	2.85	3.40	3.95	4.50	5.00
150cm fabric	0.85	1.45	2.00	2.60	3.20	3.80	4.35	4.95	5.55

No. of widths	2	3	4	5	6	7	8	9	10
Finished Length									
0.30	0.90	1.35	1.80	2.25	2.70	3.15	3.60	4.05	4.50
0.35	1.00	1.50	2.00	2.50	3.00	3.50	4.00	4.50	5.00
0.40	1.10	1.65	2.20	2.75	3.30	3.85	4.40	4.95	5.50
0.45	1.20	1.80	2.40	3.00	3.60	4.20	4.80	5.40	6.00
0.50	1.30	1.95	2.60	3.25	3.90	4.55	5.20	5.85	6.50
0.55	1.40	2.10	2.80	3.50	4.20	4.90	5.60	6.30	7.00
0.60	1.50	2.25	3.00	3.75	4.50	5.25	6.00	6.75	7.50
0.65	1.60	2.40	3.20	4.00	4.80	5.60	6.40	7.20	8.00
0.70	1.70	2.55	3.40	4.25	5.10	5.95	6.80	7.65	8.50
0.75	1.80	2.70	3.60	4.50	5.40	6.30	7.20	8.10	9.00
0.80	1.90	2.85	3.80	4.75	5.70	6.65	7.60	8.55	9.50
0.85	2.00	3.00	4.00	5.00	6.00	7.00	8.00	9.00	10.00
0.90	2.10	3.15	4.20	5.25	6.30	7.35	8.40	9.45	10.50
0.95	2.20	3.30	4.40	5.50	6.60	7.70	8.80	9.90	11.00
1.00	2.30	3.45	4.60	5.75	6.90	8.05	9.20	10.35	11.50

To use this chart:

1 Find your fabric width at top right in the first column. Go along the line to the right of the fabric width to find the nearest measurement to the width of your track or pole – if this falls between two measurements, use the larger one.

2 Find the number of fabric widths you need by looking directly below your track or pole measurement in the No. of widths line.

3 The column below the number of widths shows the amount of fabric required to achieve a finished length of valances as shown in the column on the far left.

Skills and Techniques

Fabric quantities for swags and tails

Swags

Swags can be butted together or overlapped. A small overlap creates a pronounced scallop-shaped hemline. When swags are overlapped centre to centre, the hemline forms a shallow wavy shape.

Quantities given per swag, finished depth either 45cm or 55cm
Assumes 137cm-wide fabric

Measurements in metres

Swag width	Fabric quantity (No. of widths x cut drop)	Hem measurement for fringe quantities
0.60	1.10 (1 x 1.10)	1.50
0.70	1.10 (1 x 1.10)	1.60
0.80	1.10 (1 x 1.10)	1.65
0.90	1.15 (1 x 1.15)	1.70
1.00	1.15 (1 x 1.15)	1.75
1.10	1.15 (1 x 1.15)	1.80
1.20	1.15 (1 x 1.15)	1.90
1.30	2.30 (2 x 1.15)	1.95
1.40	2.40 (2 x 1.20)	2.05
1.50	2.40 (2 x 1.20)	2.10
1.60	2.40 (2 x 1.20)	2.20
1.70	2.40 (2 x 1.20)	2.30

Tails

Quantities given per pair, 15cm pelmet board return
Assumes 137cm-wide fabric

Measurements in metres

Length of tail up to	Fabric	Contrast lining	Hem measurement for fringe quantities
0.90 – straight tail	2.00 (2 x 1.00)	2.00	2.30
1.10 – straight tail	2.40 (2 x 1.20)	2.40	2.50
1.35 – straight tail	2.90 (2 x 1.45)	2.90	3.30
1.35 – cone shape	3.30 (2 x 1.65)	3.30	3.70
1.65 – straight tail	3.50 (2 x 1.75)	3.50	3.60
1.65 – cone shape	3.90 (2 x 1.95)	3.90	4.00

Fabric quantities for Roman blinds

Roman blinds can be fitted inside or outside the window reveal and are a smart form of window dressing where wall space around the window is restricted.

15cm for heading and hem allowance
30cm of fabric to cover batten

Measurements in metres

	Finished width of blind up to	Finished width of blind up to
120cm fabric	1.10	2.20
137cm fabric	1.25	2.55
150cm fabric	1.35	2.80
	Finished length	**Finished length**
	+ 0.45	+ 0.45 x 2 widths

To use this chart:

1 Find your fabric width at top right in the first column. The first column to the right of the fabric width shows the maximum finished width blind you can make with one width of fabric, the second column shows the maxiumn finished width blind you can make with two widths.

2 To find the length of fabric required take the finished length of the blind, multiply by the number of widths of fabric required and add 45 cm for heading, hem and to cover the batten.

Sewing skills

Preparing to cut and pattern match

Take time to check you have everything you need before making a start. Double-check that you remembered to allow enough fabric for pattern repeats before cutting – see measuring section.

1 Cutting out – cut fabric on long clean surface. Check all lengths of fabric are running the same way. Use a set square and metal ruler to mark a straight line across the fabric. Measure the first drop down the selvedge line and mark your top and bottom with pins, making sure your next drop matches at repeats. Continue this way for rest of widths – part widths go on the outer edges.

2 Pattern match – put the two selvedges together and line up print facing you on both sides as in the diagram – pop a pin in at the top and bottom to hold in place as a marker.

Tips

Use a large stitch when sewing seams as a small tight seam causes pulling and puckering and doesn't always press out.

3 Pin and sew – lay your two curtain lengths down on your sewing table face to face – selvedge to selvedge. Place the pins horizontally as in the diagram. Allow 2.5cm (1in) from selvedge for sewing line for a plain fabric. If it is a print then the sewing line depends on the pattern match. Machine straight over your pins – don't worry, they won't break nor will your machine needle! If you don't believe it you can use a running stitch instead.

4 Snip seams – go quite close to machine line but not through it. Snipping stops any puckering or gathering on seams – essential when machining shaped parts of a curtain. Press seam open with a fairly hot iron.

Stitches

Running, gathering and tacking stitch
Stitch used for tacking or gathering.

Hemming stitch
Used to hem and to stop fraying.

Herringbone stitch
Used for hems or to neaten seams.

Loose stitch
Sometimes used to loosely attach lining to fabric.

Overlocking stitch
Used to stop fabric fraying on hand sewn curtains.

Blanket stitch
Use thick wool or thread for this.

Blind stitching
For sewing on ribbons and braids by hand.

Locking stitch
Used for joining interlining to the main fabric.

Unlined drapes with mitering

1 Measure the window as shown on page 264 and cut your fabric accordingly, remembering to add seam allowances for hem, headings and side seams.

2 If you are using more than one width of fabric for each curtain, pin, tack and machine stitch the widths together.

3 Overlock the edges of all seams to stop the fabric fraying—press the seams open.

4 On both sides of one curtain make a double hem by turning the edges in TWICE by 3cm (1¼in) each time. Pin and tack these edges to within 7cm (2¾in) from the top of the curtain and 15cm (6in) from the bottom.

5 Turn up the hem allowance by 15cm (6in) TWICE and press flat. Open out the folds and then fold the bottom corners across diagonally to meet the seam line to make a mitre.

6 Cut away the excess fabric across the mitre around 5mm (¼in) from the diagonal fold.

7 Fold the double hem back into place, then slip stitch the hem.

8 Turn over the top to the wrong side by enough to make the curtain the finished length required. Stitch your chosen heading tape in place across the top.

9 Knot the loose cords at one end of the heading tape and pull on the cords at the other end to gather the fabric into even pleats across the width of the curtain. Knot the cords, wind the excess around your fingers and tuck behind the heading tape. Slot the hooks onto the tape—there is usually a choice of levels, depending on whether you are hanging the curtain from a pole or a track. Repeat steps 4 to 9 for the other curtain.

Locked-in Lining

1 Make up the curtain as described above.

2 Lock-stitch is used on hand-made curtains to attach a separate lining loosely to the main fabric. The lining is laid on the curtain with wrong sides together (both already hemmed). The leading edge is hemmed, then, at 45cm (18in) intervals across the width, the lining is folded back. From the top almost to the bottom of the lining, a long, loose stitch is made catching the curtain and then the lining. This is followed by a small back-stitch on lining.

Lined drapes

1 Measure, cut and make up your main curtain fabric as in steps 1–3 on page 272.

2 Cut the lining the same size as your finished curtains will be (in other words DO NOT ADD ANY SEAM ALLOWANCES AT THE SIDES, OR ALLOWANCES FOR HEADING OR HEM!).

3 If you are using more than one width of fabric for each curtain lining, pin tack and machine stitch all of the widths together.

4 Make a double hem on the lining, turning the hem up by 3cm (1¼in) each time, then machine the hem and press. Press under the raw edges by 2.5cm (1in) on the sides and top of the lining only.

5 Place the lining centrally onto the curtain with right sides together. Pin into position and then stitch the seams on each side only.

6 Turn the curtain right side out and press down the side seams.

7 Turn up the hem allowance twice on the main curtain fabric by 15cm (6in) each time and press flat. Open out and then press the two corners to the seam line to make a mitre.

8 Slip stitch the hem. Add your chosen heading tape as in steps 8 and 9 on page 272. Repeat steps 4 to 8 to line the other curtain.

Tips

To stop the lining flapping around behind the curtain, you can always put a loose chain stitch here and there.

Tie heading

1 Cut out the fabric for the curtains and the ties – which should each be about 2.5cm (1in) wide and 20cm (8in) long.

2 Make the curtains as for unlined curtains, steps 1 to 8 (see page 272) but do not add heading tape.

3 Make the ties by pressing the fabric in half and then in quarters. Press in the short ends and machine stitch all around the ties. Fold each tie in half.

4 Lay the curtain fabric down with the right side facing upwards and lay the folded ties equally spaced apart across the top. Pin the ties in place.

5 Cut a strip of fabric the width of one curtain and about 10cm (4in) deep as a facing and turn under all the edges. Place the facing along the top edge of the curtain, covering the base of the ties, and stitch around to hold the ties in place. Repeat steps 4 and 5 on the other curtain.

Tab heading

1 Cut out the main fabric for the curtains and the tabs.

2 Cut the facing for both curtains – a strip of fabric the width of the curtain and about 10cm (4in) deep.

3 Make the curtains as for unlined curtains steps 1 to 8 (see page 272) but do not add heading tape.

4 Make the tabs by cutting a length of fabric about 20cm (8in) long for each. Fold in half lengthways, right sides together, and stitch. Turn the tube right side out.

5 Fold each tab in half and lay at equal intervals along the top edge of the curtain, with folds pointing down. Tack in place.

6 Lay the facing on top, wrong sides together and with edges turned under. Slip stitch the facing all around to neaten.

Italian stringing

1 Put up your pole and fix the cleat about one-third of the way up from the floor.

2 Cut the top and contrast fabrics for the curtain to the same size with usual top, hem and side seam allowances.

3 Lay the top and the contrast right sides together. Pin, tack and then machine stitch together leaving just the top open to form a 'bag'. Turn the curtain right side out through the top and press the seams.

4 To apply the heading tape, fold down the top of the curtain by about 3cm (1¼in). Check your required length and if the curtain is too long or short adjust the fold here to achieve the correct length. Pin the chosen heading tape

1cm (½in) from the top. Tack and then machine stitch in place. Tie a knot in the cords of the tape and gather the curtain to the required width, and then tie a bow with the long cords. Make sure the pleats are even across the top.

5 Sew braid onto leading edge of the curtain.

6 Place the curtain right side down. Sew a cording ring on the contrast fabric at the leading edge, about one-third of the way down the curtain. Sew another four or five rings to the contrast fabric running at a 45° angle towards the other edge of the curtain, about 20cm (8in) apart. Knot the cord onto the first ring and thread through the other rings – leave plenty of cord at the end to secure into a cleat on the wall.

7 Wind the loose cords of the heading tape around your fingers and tuck behind the end of the tape. Hang the curtain in place, then pull up the stringing cord to pull the edge of the curtain into an attractive curving shape. Secure the loose cord to the cleat on the wall.

Tips

Don't use a very heavy fabric for the curtains as the stringing is not that strong.

Skills and Techniques

Valance on a pelmet board

1 Cover the pelmet board—put into place together with the curtain track.

2 Staple the first side of the touch and close tape to the front of the pelmet board.

3 Cut the main curtain fabric to your measurements and make up as on page 273 (lined curtains). Put on heading tape as in steps 8 and 9 on page 272. Press, then put on your curtain hooks and hang the curtains.

4 Measure the actual width of the pelmet board plus the returns (sides) and cut a template in paper to this width. As a guide for the depth of your valance, cut the deepest section to about half the length of your main curtains. Fold the paper template in half to find the centre line and then shape the bottom edge with a dotted line. Tack your template to the pelmet and check the proportions – adjust accordingly.

5 To make an elongated template for the fabric, simply multiply the actual width of the pelmet by 2.5 and add on the returns. Now take the centre measurement off the original template and transfer this to the centre of the elongated one; do the same at both ends and continue to take measurements at regular intervals, say every 10cm (4in). Then all you need to do is join up the dots and you have a shaped valance template (see diagrams on page 277 for examples).

Tips

Before you continue, look at the page opposite, where you will find some valance templates. When you have studied these and made your choice – proceed!

6 Pin your finished template on to your fabric and, remembering to add your seam allowances top and bottom, make a dotted line around the shape. Cut out – then repeat for lining. Press the seam allowances to the wrong side along all edges of the main fabric, clipping any curves and mitring the corners. Open out the top hem and stitch a strip of buckram underneath, then fold back. Pin and slip stitch the hems in place. Turn under the seam allowances around all edges of the lining, centre it over the valance, wrong sides together, and slip stitch in place along all edges.

7 Work out how many goblets you will need for your valance width – as a guide I allow about 15cm (6in) for each goblet and the same for each gap between them. With the right side of the fabric facing you, fold over your 15cm (6in) pleat, tack and machine to just below the bottom edge of the buckram. Then secure the base of each goblet with a few stitches. Open up each goblet to make a 'cup' and stuff with wadding.

8 Sew on the fan edge trim. Knot and loop the rope at the base of the goblets. Stitch the other side of the touch and close tape to the back of the fabric about 2.5cm (1in) from the top and press the valance into place.

Valance templates

REMEMBER if the valances are gathered you must elongate the shapes to allow for the fabric fullness, so you will need to cut a second template to the finished size of the actual valance before gathering. Then you need to take the measurements indicated and transfer to the main diagram in order to arrive at the correct shape.

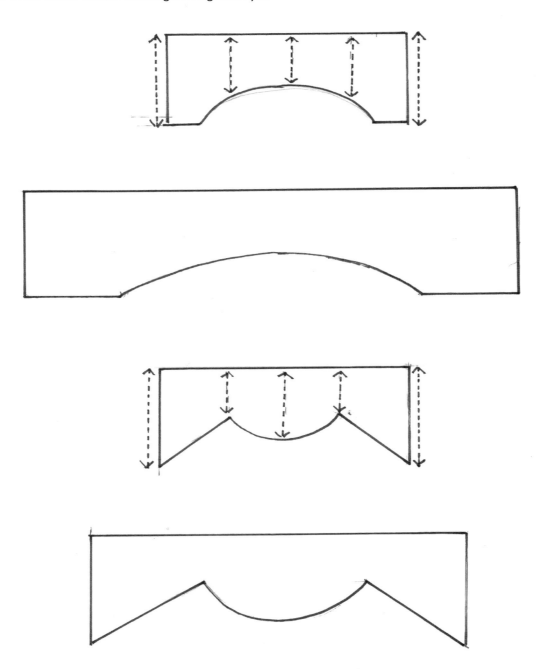

Roman shades

1 Cut your fabric to the exact size of the blind plus seam allowances – and the same for the lining.

2 Cover the pelmet board with matching fabric.

3 Staple a length of one half of the touch and close tape to the front edge of the pelmet board (see step 2 page 276).

4 Put the pelmet board in its place with the correct brackets.

5 Work on your main fabric first – press the sides and the bottom turnings under once, then put the main fabric to one side.

6 Press in the side turnings on the lining so it is about 5cm (2in) narrower than the main fabric.

7 Mark your lining with tailor's chalk exactly where you need the pockets for the dowel rods. As a rough guide, measure 10cm (4in) up from the bottom and that is where the first pocket should be – then one every 25–30cm (10–12in). Make sure they are evenly distributed. Make your pockets by folding strips of fabric the width of the blind in half and then into quarters.

8 Machine each of the dowel rod pockets onto the lining in turn. Slide rounded wooden dowels into each pocket. To make up the blind, carefully slip stitch the lining to the main fabric along the sides and bottom.

9 Add small brass rings to the edge of each pocket, in a line near each side of the blind. Screw two eyelet screws onto the underside of the pelmet board in line with the brass rings on the blind. Turn over the raw edge at the top of the blind and slip stitch a length of the second half of the touch and close tape to hide the raw edge. Press the tape to the length on the pelmet board to hang the blind.

10 Lastly, thread the cord through the rings as in the diagram – the diagram is from the window looking into the room, so is for a left hand pull blind – and thread the cord end onto the cord, before wrapping the cord around a cleat on the wall to secure.

Oriental shades

1 Cut the fabric the length of your window plus 25cm (10in) for the hems and 5cm (2in) for the sides.

2 Lay the fabric wrong side up and make a double hem down the sides by pressing under 0.5cm (¼in) and then another 3cm (1¼in).

3 Make a double hem at the top of the blind, turning under by 10cm (4in) and then another 10cm (4in). Press, tack and machine.

4 Mark your two sets of eyelet holes – place the outer set 5cm (2in) down from the top and 15cm (6in) from one side. The inner hole should be 10cm (4in) in from this one. Repeat on the other side.

5 Punch the four holes with a fairly large size eyelet hole.

6 Place the dowel rod along the bottom, turn the raw edge of the blind under then fold it over the dowel and staple in place.

7 Slip stitch a length of the looped half of the touch and close tape to the reverse side of the top of the blind. Cover the batten with fabric, then attach the batten to its correct position over the window with long screws. Staple the other half of the touch and close tape to the batten.

8 Screw the two eyelet screws onto the underside of the batten in line with the two outer eyelet holes on the blind. Attach the blind with the two sides of the touch and close tape. Now thread your cord starting from the cleat—just follow the arrows above.

Patterns for basic table covers

Plain

1 Measure your table from the centre to the floor – double the measurement and add seam allowances. Lay your fabric on a flat surface – your fabric may be wide enough to cut the full circle, but if not then follow the diagram below.

2 Once you have drawn your circle, cut the extra fabric and seam onto the edge of the main fabric as shown.

3 Press a double hem all the way around and, finally, machine the edge carefully.

Top and undercover

1 Make the undercover as for a plain table cover.

2 For the top cover, cut the fabric into a square. Press a double hem all around.

3 Mitre the corners as on page 272 and tack. Lastly, machine all around the square and press.

Square

1 Take the measurements of the pieces shown in the diagrams below and draw the pieces on a piece of graph paper – allow a seam allowance on every edge.

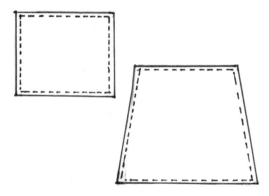

2 Pin, tack and sew together and cut away any excess fabric in the corners.

Glossary

abutted seam – a seam used to join non-woven interfacing, in which the two edges are butted together over a narrow band of lightweight fabric underlay and a line of wide zigzag machine stitching down the join holds the two pieces together.

anchor – to fix the end of a piece of yarn or thread, or attach a piece of fabric at one point, so it will not pull away from the main piece. Some stitchers begin sewing with a few small running stitches to anchor the thread, others prefer to knot the end so that it will not pull through the fabric.

architrave – a moulded frame around the sides and top of a window or door.

bias strip or binding – a strip of fabric cut on a 45° diagonal to the straight of grain of a piece of fabric. It is used to bind edges, particularly curved edges. It stretches very easily and should be handled with care.

blackout lining – a lining of closely woven fabric, or a plastic-coated fabric, that will block the passage of light. Also known as a light-resistant lining.

blend – a fabric that is a mixture of two materials, such as polyester/cotton, or mohair/wool. The mix can be 50/50 or may be unequal amounts, such as 50 percent merino wool/33 percent microfibre/12 percent cashmere. The exact composition of fabric is usually given on the end of the bolt.

bolt – an amount of fabric, wound onto a round tube or a flattened oval cardboard form. The fabric is usually folded lengthways, right sides together and the amount in a bolt depends on the type of fabric and the manufacturer. Wholesale fabric stores often sell fabric by the bolt, rather than by cut length, so you purchase a larger amount but at a cheaper price per metre/yard.

box valance – a three-dimensional valance that has sides and a front and protrudes from the wall above a curtain, covering the curtain heading. *See also* valance, pelmet.

buckram – a stiffened hessian-like fabric, used to stiffen pelmets and curtain headings.

bullion fringe – a thick, heavy and long fringe.

butting – bringing two edges together so that they touch but do not overlap.

canopy – fabric draped or hung over a frame attached to a four-poster bed, or a decorative treatment above a headboard. *See also* corona, half tester.

catch – to attach one piece of fabric to another, generally with a few tiny backstitches made by hand. For instance, a facing could be attached to a seam allowance.

clip – to cut a short distance into a seam allowance or selvedge with the point of the scissors. It is used on curved seams, square corners and in similar places, to remove excess fabric so seams will lie flat when pressed.

colourway – any of a range of combinations of colours in which a style or design is available.

composition – the percentage of each material that a fabric is made from. This is generally given on the end of the bolt, but may also be printed or woven in the selvedge. It is important to know the composition so you will know how to treat the finished item when it needs cleaning or pressing.

corona – a decorative half-circular frame above the head of a bed, that often supports a canopy. *See also* canopy, half tester.

count – the number of warp and weft fabric threads in an inch of fabric. It is used to indicate the fineness or coarseness of a fabric.

covered lathe – a decorative strip hiding a curtain track when the curtains are open.

cut length – the cut length is a piece of fabric that has been measured and cut. In curtains, it is the length to cut for each width, allowing for the matching of repeats.

directional designs – see one-way designs.

drape – the property of a fabric to fall into folds. If it falls gracefully it is said to drape well or have good drape.

dress curtain – a curtain that is for show and is not intended – or is not able – to be drawn across the window.

dressed curtain – a curtain that has had its folds adjusted into even lines and then loosely tied and left to 'set', so that when the ties are removed the folds will remain in place. Formal curtains should always be dressed – and dress curtains are usually dressed.

drop/finished drop – the measurement from the top to the bottom of a completely finished curtain, with all seams and hems stitched in place.

Glossary

eyelet – small round hole in fabric, which may be hand-stitched or created with a punch and lined with a metal ring that grips the fabric on the reverse. Hand-stitched eyelets are edged with overcast stitching or blanket stitch to stop the edges fraying. Eyelets are used for curtain headings, for decorative effect and to take lacing.

facing – a shaped piece of fabric stitched on the seam line and turned inside to create a finished edge.

finial – turned shape used to end a pole decoratively.

flush window – a window that is set level with the front face of a wall.

four-poster – type of bed with a flat 'ceiling' of fabric – or sometimes wood – that covers the entire bed area and is supported by full-height posts that extend upwards from each corner of the bed. Sometimes it also has curtains that can be draw right around to enclose the bed. Also called a tester. *See also* half tester, canopy, corona.

frill – a ruffled, gathered or pleated border also known as a ruffle.

fullness – an amount of extra fabric allowed across the width of a curtain, so it will still have gathers or pleats even when pulled closed across the window.

gathering – a method of controlling fullness by running a double line of large stitches through a fabric, fastening the threads at one end and pulling on the other end to reduce the fabric to a smaller length.

gimp – narrow flat braid or rounded cord of fabric used for trimming or as the base of other trimmings.

grain – this is the direction of the threads making up a woven fabric, so each piece has two – lengthways (warp) and widthways or crosswise (weft).

half-drop repeat – with a half-drop repeat, the motifs repeat across the fabric, but on alternate lines they are offset so each motif falls in the centre between the motifs above and below. *See also* pattern repeat.

half tester – A half tester has a 'ceiling' that extends only partway down the bed, cantilevered from above the head end, so the bed does not have full-height foot posts. *See also* tester, canopy, corona.

heading – the top of a curtain or valance.

hold-back – a solid hoop or decorative knob that is fixed to the wall on each side of a curtain. When open, the curtain is hooked back behind the hold-back to hold it in place. *See also* tie-back.

interlining – a non-woven brushed fabric placed between the lining and the main fabric of a curtain to add body, insulation and to help the fabric fold properly.

Italian stringing – a method of opening curtains in which the curtains are fixed at the top, but cording running diagonally across the curtain pulls it up from near the bottom into a deep curve towards the top.

leading edge – the edge of a curtain that travels across the window.

lambrequins – a flat ornamental drapery across the top and down the side of a window or door, or suspended from the edge of a shelf.

lengthways fold – a fold down the length of a piece of fabric. Very wide fabric on a bolt is generally folded lengthways, with right sides together.

light-resistant lining – see blackout lining.

mitre – a diagonal join between two strips of fabric meeting at a square corner.

nap – fabric with nap usually has a short pile and will look different shades from different angles because it catches the light differently. Velvet and velour are both fabrics with nap. When making curtains with a napped fabric, make sure that the pile runs the same way on each width.

neaten – to finish off by pulling loose threads to the wrong side and tying or stitching them in before cutting off. Seam edges can be neatened and prevented from fraying by binding, pinking or zigzag stitching.

one-way designs – designs based on repeating motifs with a distinct top and bottom, so they run in only one direction and will look very different if the fabric is turned upside down. Also called directional designs. When making curtains with a one-way fabric, make sure that the design is running the same way on each width.

overlap – the amount the leading edge of one curtain overlaps the leading edge of other curtain.

panel – flat fabric which is lined only, with weights in the hem to make it hang straight. The panel is then hung from tracking, which is generally attached to the ceiling.

pattern repeat – most patterns are made up of one or more components that repeat along the length and/or width. The length of a pattern repeat is determined by measuring from a set point on a motif to the matching point on the next. In a full drop repeat the rows are all repeated with the motifs directly in line both down and across. *See also* half-drop repeat.

pelmet – a solid covering that hides the top of a curtain. It may be carved, fretwork, moulded or covered in fabric.

pin tuck – a very narrow stitched tuck in fabric. Several are often made in close parallel rows to give a decorative look. *See also* tuck.

pleat – even folds in fabric to add fullness.

portière – a one-sided curtain that acts as a door in a corridor, or a window/door covering with slotted rods at top and bottom that are attached to the wall at one end only, so the panel can swing open.

raw edge – a cut edge of fabric that has not been finished in any way.

recessed window – a window that is set back into an alcove in the wall.

repeat – see pattern repeat.

return – part of the curtain that returns to the wall at the end of the curtain rail – also applies to the outer edge of a pelmet or valance.

right side – in printed fabrics the pattern will be clearer and brighter on the right side, but the difference is not always so obvious. The term is usually abbreviated to RS.

saddle stitching – a decorative form of stitching done with two needles, where each stitch butts right up to the following one.

seam allowance – the amount of fabric allowed for seams when joining two pieces of fabric together. Usually there is a seam allowance of 1.5cm (⅝in), between the cutting line and the seamline.

selvedge – this is the finished edge along either side of the length of fabric. These edges will not fray, but it is usually better to avoid incorporating them into curtains as they sometimes pucker up when the fabric is laundered.

slub – an uneven thread or yarn with thicker sections, which may be accidental or by design. When woven the fabric will have random nubs running with the weave. With some fabrics, such as slubbed silk, this is an essential part of the character of the fabric.

stack back – the width of the hung curtain when it is pulled completely open.

straight of grain – threads running lengthways, or parallel to the selvedges, are on the straight of grain. Threads running widthways, or from selvedge to selvedge, are on the cross grain.

swags – a graceful fold of fabric across the top of a window. Often combined with tails.

swatch – small piece of fabric, used as a colour sample.

tacking – a technique used to temporarily hold layers of fabric together for fitting or to stop them slipping as seams are stitched. The US term is basting.

tails – ends of fabric that hang down in decorative folds at each side of a window. Often combined with a swag.

tie-back – a short decorative length of fabric, cording or rope that is either hooked or fixed to the wall and is used to tie back a curtain when it is in the open position.

touch and close tape – a type of fastening that comes in two parts; one half has tiny loops and the other tiny hooks so when pressed together they cling to each other. It is often used for items that need to be unfastened quickly. Also known as hook and loop tape; in the UK it is known as Velcro®.

tuck – stitched fold of fabric, often used as a decorative feature. See also pin tuck.

valance – a soft draped or gathered fabric covering to the top of a curtain.

width – the measurement across a piece of fabric. A curtain may be made up of several widths to enable it to cover a window with some fullness.

wrong side – the side of a fabric that will not be seen. In printed fabrics the pattern will be fainter and duller on the wrong side, but the difference is not always so obvious. The term is usually abbreviated to WS.

Index

About the Author

If you don't know my name or have not seen any of my previous books, then let me tell you a little bit about myself, and my work. I was born in London rather a long time ago. My father was in the Navy during the war and afterwards went to work on the *Evening Standard*. My mother was the daughter of a Court Dressmaker, which is perhaps why I went into the 'rag trade' at the start of my working life. She was my guide, my tower of strength and she filled me with determination...I miss her to bits!

I left school at 15 and went to business college for a year, against my wishes – my mother was determined I should be a secretary. I ran away from home at 16 and bought a one way ticket to the furthest point £25 would take me: Rome. I worked as a model in Europe for several years, but eventually I came home to London.

It was the height of the sixties and I opened a boutique in Kensington under the name of Harriet – and that is what everyone called me for 18 years. I was clubbing by night and working by day – life was such fun. Harriet soon expanded and we moved from Kensington High Street to the real 'rag trade' area, Margaret Street. Soon Harriet was in all the major department stores in London and New York. Life was busy – but tiring, and by this time I was married and had my wonderful daughter and I wanted to spend time with her. So I went on holiday for 10 days. I came back bored out of my mind and realised I needed to work!

I was looking for a new challenge when my best friend, Jean, asked if I would pay for her to train as a beauty therapist. When she qualified she asked if I would like to go into business with her. I wasn't really interested in beauty therapies, but liked the idea of running a beauty salon so we opened Secrets a few months later. The combination of my business brain and Jean's natural flair meant we were an instant success, but I found that I hated the beauty business, so I decided to move on.

Being an interior designer seemed to be all the rage in the eighties, and I decided to give that a go. So there I was, with a big pile of carpet samples and lots of fabrics. I put an advert in *House and Garden* and sat by the telephone until one day I got my first client. Whatever I didn't know I made up as I went along and I never looked back. After a few years I had a big client list, including many well-known faces and many multi-national companies.

My first sketchbook of curtain designs was just a few rough sketches put together with a paperclip – it was useful for me to have in my bag to show clients a few of my ideas. It was always a problem trying to explain how a covered lathe worked, or which way the curtains would pull in a bay window. The sketchbook saved me having to draw things afresh for each individual client.

Soon other designers heard about my sketchbook and they began to ask for a copy. Six months later my husband set up a desk in the garage where he collated the pages before taking them to be laminated. The first Sketchbooks were collections of single laminated pages and cost £35 each... we sold thousands of them!

For some years I lived in France, but now I am home in England and glad to be. I live with my companion Dawson and I have a wonderful daughter who is an amazing photographer and who fills me with joy. I always try to keep all my books up to date, and I make sure that if there is a new trend in US or Europe it is shown in my books as soon as possible. The Sketchbooks keep selling and I keep working as a designer and writer... but I have a few new ideas up my sleeve, so watch this space!

I would like to thank Chrissie Carriere for her wonderful illustrations, Holly Jolliffe for the photography, Malena Burgess for the styling and all the fabric companies and suppliers listed below.

Picture credits: pp. 2, 6, 72, 108 and 148 courtesy of Designers Guild (www.designersguild.com, 020 7893 7400); pp. 26, 46, 64, 176 and 248 courtesy of Osborne and Little (www.osborneandlittle.com, 020 7352 1456); p. 70 courtesy of Byron & Byron (www.byronandbyron.com, 020 8344 7979); p.210 courtesy of And So To Bed (www.andsotobed.co.uk, 0808 144 4343). All other photography by Holly Jolliffe.

Fabric swatches: p.18 L–R Alton-Brooke, Colefax & Fowler, Jane Churchill, Parkertex, Colefax & Fowler, Zimmer & Rohde, Colefax & Fowler, Mulberry; p.19 L–R Osborne & Little, Romo, Designers Guild, Manuel Canovas, Colefax & Fowler, Alton-Brooke, Designers Guild, Designers Guild, Alton-Brooke; p.20 L–R Colefax & Fowler, Nina Campbell/Osborne & Little, Romo, Osborne & Little, Malabar, GP&J Baker, Romo, Malabar; p.21 L–R Manuel Canovas, Manuel Canovas, Jane Churchill, Lorca, Designers Guild, Colefax & Fowler, Sheila Coombes, Sheila Coombes; p.22 L–R Designers Guild, Lorca, Manuel Canovas, J. Robert Scott, Jane Churchill, Lorca, Jane Churchill, Designers Guild, Zimmer & Rohde; p.23 L–R Kravet, Osborne & Little, Designers Guild, Designers Guild, Zimmer & Rohde, Designers Guild, Kravet.

Wendy Baker
London 2008